Dedication

For the past five years, the art new media staff of the *American River Review* has been fortunate to share each class with an adviser who leads through example. A gifted artist himself, his passion for art and design is shared in a fun and stress-free environment.

He mentors his students, and for many, he is a favorite teacher. His attitude is always upbeat and positive and he is a source of knowledge and experience.

He inspires his students, encouraging them to stay in school and stay focused. He helps them refine their skills and encourages exploration and experimentation with new techniques. His own work ethic motivates others to follow his lead.

Treating students as peers and friends, he creates a positive atmosphere using humor and sensitivity. For many staff members, this has their best college experience, and their fond memories will last far into the future.

The 2015 *American River Review* is dedicated to artist, teacher, inspiration, and friend, Professor Craig Martinez.

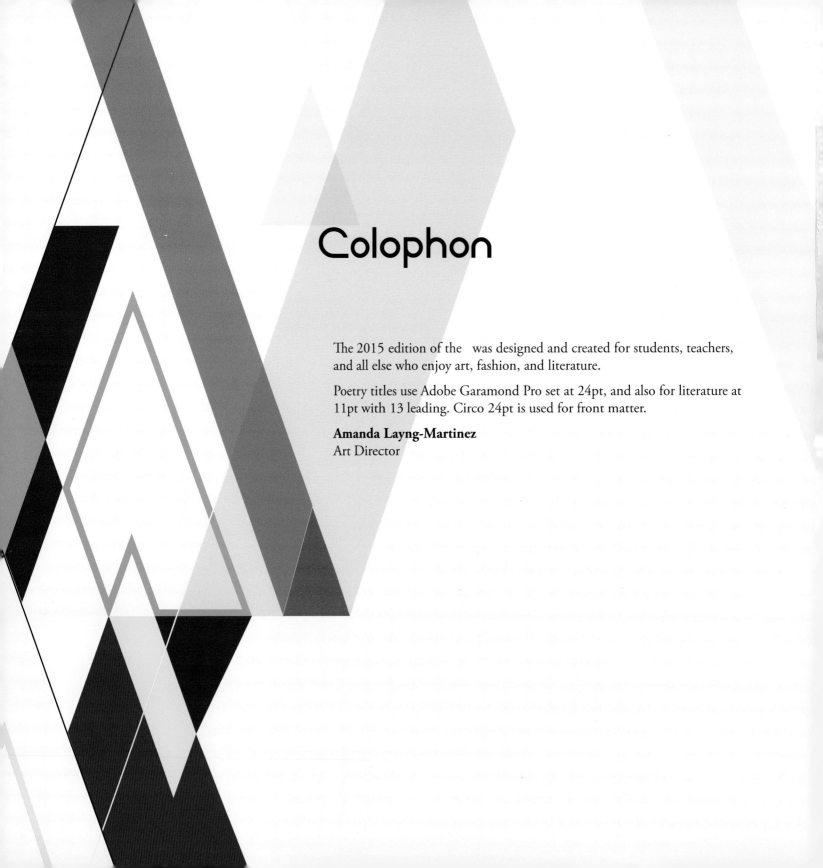

Colophon

The 2015 edition of the   was designed and created for students, teachers, and all else who enjoy art, fashion, and literature.

Poetry titles use Adobe Garamond Pro set at 24pt, and also for literature at 11pt with 13 leading. Circo 24pt is used for front matter.

Amanda Layng-Martinez
Art Director

Art Gallery

Amy K. Larson
Rusted
Film, Digital
17x11 Inches

Amy K. Larson
Three
Film, Digital
11x17 Inches

Louis Archuleta
Beauty Beneath Ash
Photography
20x13 Inches

Louis Archuleta
Restless
Photography
9x13 Inches

7

Christl Clinton
Untitled
Cyanotype Over Brown Print
8x10 Inches

Melanie Scott
Shy Ghost
Oil on Canvas
14x11 Inches

Kyle Doka
Untitled
Ink Jet Print
8x10 Inches

David Navarro
Raley's Man
Digital Photography
24x20 Inches

Kyle Doka
Untitled
Ink Jet Print
8x10 Inches

David Navarro
Plain Dream
Digital
20x13.375 Inches

Christl Clinton
Untitled
Photography
8x10 Inches

Christl Clinton
Untitled
Photography
8x10 Inches

11

Cathie Bechtell
Untitled
Photography
8x10 Inches

Victoria Kozycz
Silhouette
Photography
11x17 Inches

Dakota Arguello
Hold On
Oil
16x20x1/2 Inches

Denise Kibbe-Phillips
Free Flow
Charcoal
22x15 Inches

Armin Masoumi
Robody
Maya
35.6x20 Inches

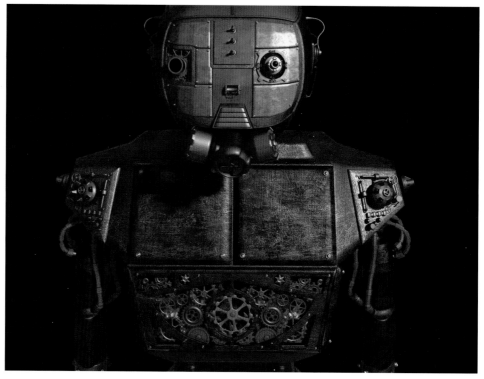

Armin Masoumi
Untitled
Maya
28.4x21.3 Inches

Hanna Benedychuk
I Am On-line
Oil
20x16 Inches

Hanna Benedychuk
Temple Of Rain
Oil
16x12 Inches

Michael Fullilove
Herculanean Turnaround
Digital
11x17 Inches

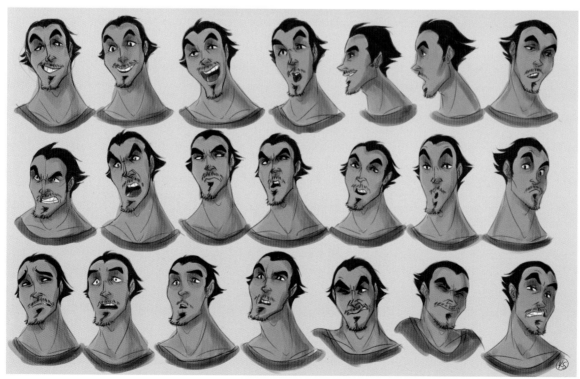

Kaila Sanfilippo
Yuigo Expression Sheet
Digital
6.853x11.05 Inches

Michael Fullilove
Vesuvius Turnaround
Digital
11x17 Inches

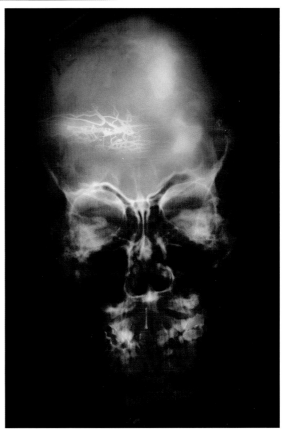

Maren McCallister
Red Skull
Digital
11x14 Inches

17

Eva Mae Natividad
Self-Portrait with
My Sister
Pastel on Paper
19x25 Inches

Ulysses Unzueta
Hurry Up, Kid!
Digital
8x4.5 Inches

Kaila Sanfilippo
Untitled
Digital
8x29.973 Inches

AP   "REFLECTION"   SPOIRIER

Susan Poirier
Reflection
Woodblock Print
10x10 Inches

Eva Mae Natividad
Pomegranates on a Green Glass Plate
Pastel on Paper
17x17 Inches

21

Jordan Siangco
The Fugitive
Line Block Print
24x18 Inches

22

J. Costa
Lonesome Cowboy
Print Relief
24x18 Inches

Matthew Beltran
Not a Docked Yacht
Print Relief
18x24 Inches

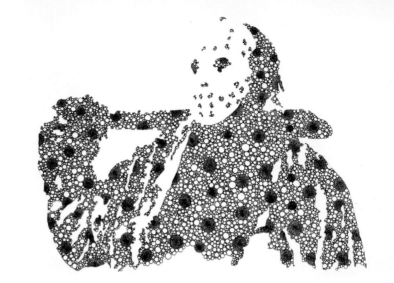

Kyla Lewis
Frank
Pen on Bristol
11x14 Inches

Kyla Lewis
Jason
Pen on Bristol
11x14 Inches

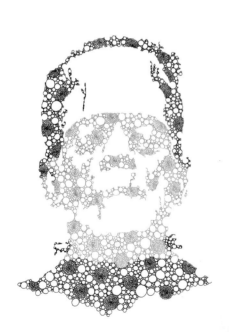

Jonathan Horcasitas
Untitled
Pen on Paper
7-1/2x5-1/2 Inches

Jonathan Horcasitas
Untitled
Pen on Paper
8-1/2x7 Inches

Penny Hanscom

1. *Northern California Coast*
Fabric
51x32 Inches

2. *Remembering the Masters: Edward Lear (1812-1888)*
There Was an Old Man with a Beard
Fabric
12x24 Inches

3. *Where's Ai WeiWei?*
Fabric
18x24 Inches

2

3

2

1

Contra

1. *Pusillanimous Blush Fluctuation*
Watercolor, Color Pencil, Markers on Paper
12x19 Inches

2. *Alternate Realm Reach*
Watercolor, Color Pencil, Markers on Paper
7x10-1/4 Inches

3 *Path of Ascension*
Spray Paint, Acrylics, Watercolor, Color Pencil
on Wood
30x48 Inches

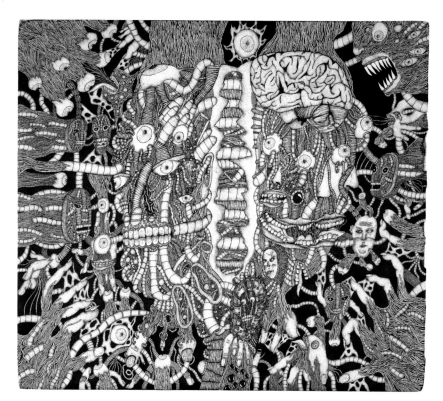

Slave
Dreams of Infamy: Oblivious Reality
Pen on Cardboard
26x23-1/2 Inches

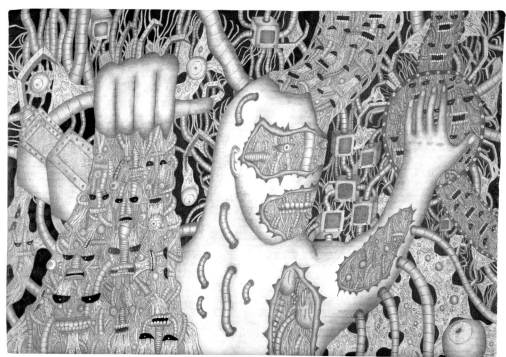

Slave
Dreams of Infamy:
Accentuate with Falsity
Black Pencil on Cardboard
25x17 Inches

Jude Croxford
Dragon Bass
Oil on Canvas
18x24 Inches

Jude Croxford
Mother Bass
Oil on Wood
24x32 Inches

Simon Tafoya
Nymph
Mixed Media on
Canvas
16x25-1/2 Inches

Kaila Sanfilippo
Grey's House
Digital
5.71x11 Inches

Cheri
Railroad
Mixed Media
9.725x9.833 Inches

Liam Byrd-Smith
Mendocino Scene
Colored Pencil on Paper
12x9 Inches

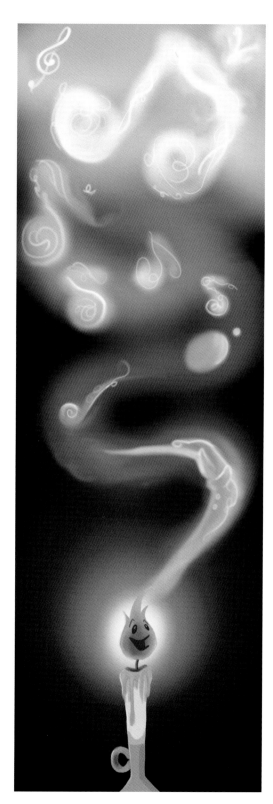

Jonathan Horcasitas
Untitled
Pen and Markers on Paper
6-1/2x8-3/4 Inches

Zach Winn
The Candle's Symphony
Digital
30x10 Inches

Thomas McFall
Intro to 3D Modeling Showcase
Maya
3.6x6.4 Inches

Philip Morgan
Intro to 3D Modeling Showcase
Maya
3.6x6.4 Inches

35

Jessica Tietjen
Grey Foxes
Acrylic
48x24x3/4 Inches

Jessie Tietjen
Black Bear
Acrylic
24x18x3/4 Inches

Antony Galvan
Gears of Time(red)
Mixed Media on Paper
18x24 Inches

Graham Fredenburg
Untitled
Clay
9x5x5 Inches

Graham Fredenburg
Jar
Porcelain
7-1/2x6-1/2x6-1/2 Inches

Sarah Martinez
Vagina Missle
Ceramic
21x11x10 Inches

Paja Lynhiavue
Escape
Chalk on Poster Paper
24x72 Inches

Sue Kelly
Majestic
Clay, Multi Fired with Slips and Oxides
18x12 Inches

Sue Kelly
Shea Shea
Clay, Raku Fired
11x9 Inches

Graham Fredenburg
Bottle
Porcelain
7x5x5 Inches

Sue Kelly
Hare on Alert
Clay, High Fired
25x13 Inches

41

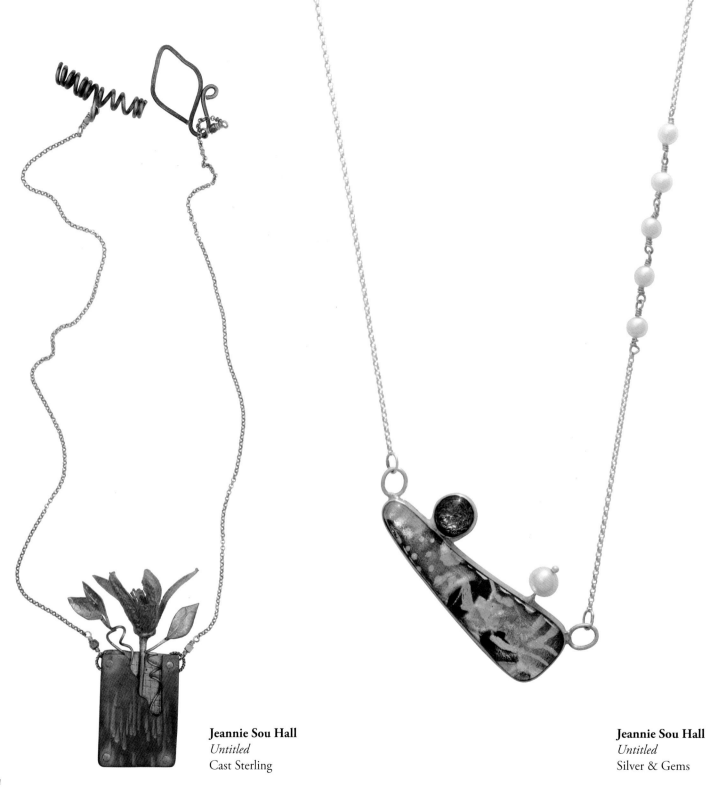

Jeannie Sou Hall
Untitled
Cast Sterling

Jeannie Sou Hall
Untitled
Silver & Gems

Elizabeth Xedes
Peony
Oil Resin
7x7 Inches

Elizabeth Xedes
Barn Owl
Wood Burning
8x7 Inches

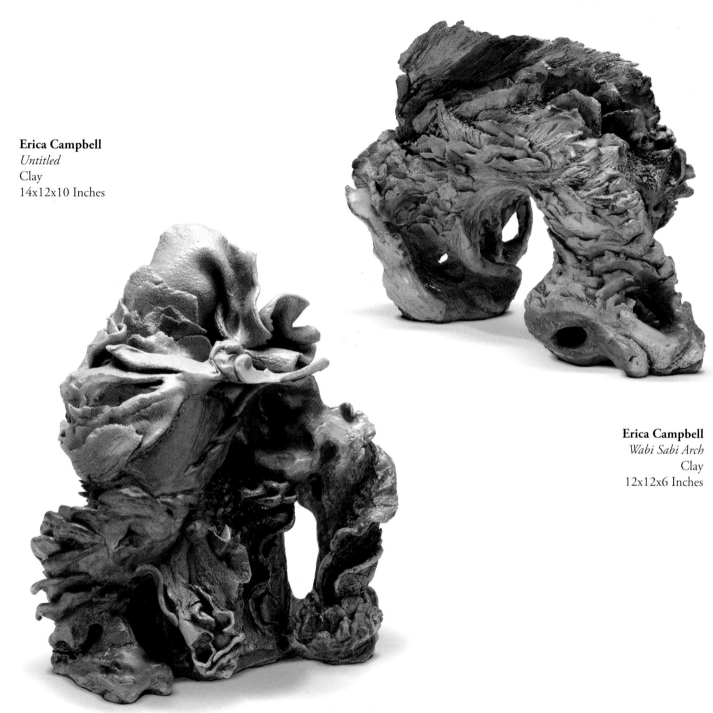

Erica Campbell
Untitled
Clay
14x12x10 Inches

Erica Campbell
Wabi Sabi Arch
Clay
12x12x6 Inches

44

Sarah Martinez
Untitled
Ceramic
12x11x4 Inches

Jeannie Sou Hall
Untitled
Cast Sterling Copper

45

Yuk Mui Michelle Wong
Untitled
Ceramic
4x4x4 Inches

Yuk Mui Michelle Wong
Untitled
Ceramic
6x3x3 Inches

Cecelia Sayer
Man 9 the Forest
Clay
11x8x8 Inches

Nancy Z'berg-Jennings
Leukothea
Ceramic
54x16x9 Inches

47

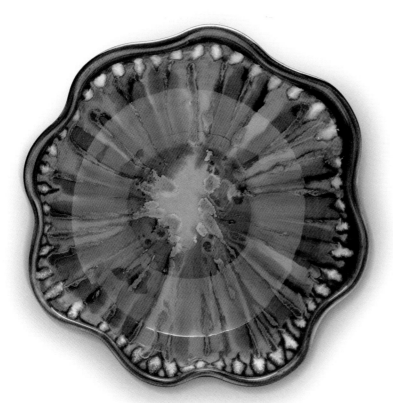

Edris Tauber
Flower Bowl
Clay
3x8 Inches

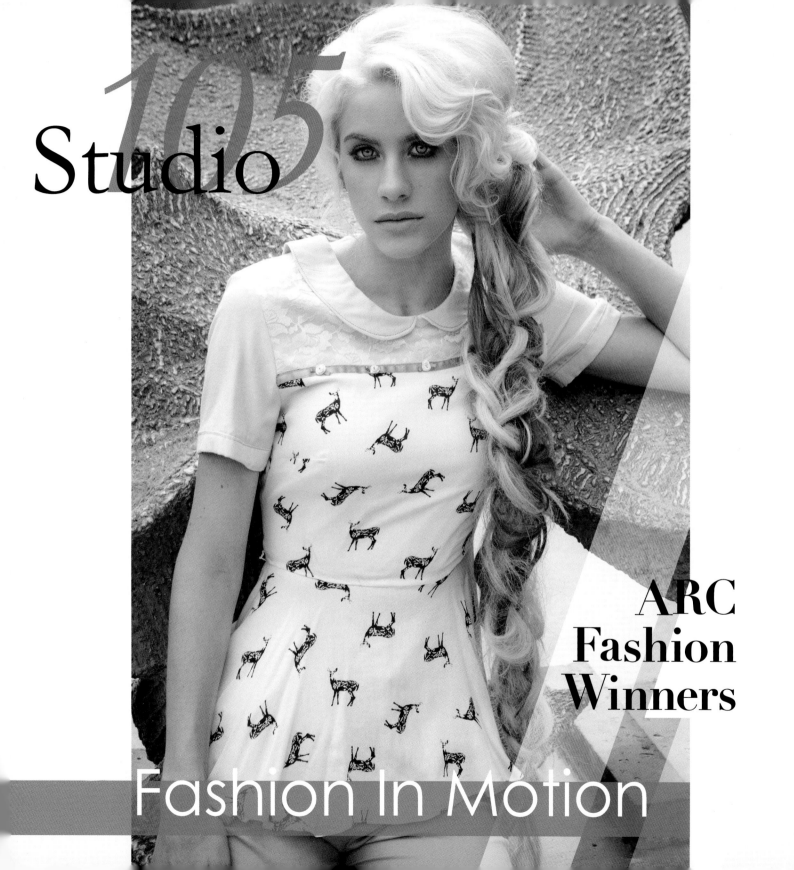

Studio 105

ARC
Fashion
Winners

Fashion In Motion

Dedication

For the past five years, the literary staff of the *American River Review* has been fortunate to share each class with an adviser who leads through example. A gifted writer himself, he skillfully guides student editors to a greater understanding of style, voice, and the challenging yet intimate connections between reader, editor, and writer.

He mentors the editors, and when they read submitted work, he knows the exact moment to ask, "What if?" What if the line break went here? What if this is really a lyric essay? What if the characters mean something entirely different than what they are actually saying?

Acting as a colleague during discussions, his questions can turn a tepid conversation into an animated debate. He inspires his students to ask these same questions, leading to the exploration of creative thought and expression.

Treating students as peers and friends, he creates an atmosphere where civil disagreement and mutual respect are consistent due to a continuing tradition of fairness, loyalty, and confidence. Because of this, many staff members have forged bonds of friendship that will last far into the future.

The 2015 *American River Review* is dedicated to writer, mentor, colleague, and friend, Professor Michael Spurgeon.

Prologue

Readers, writers, and artists seek connection, an understanding, or at the very least, a simple beauty, a tiny thread of hope. We search for a shared narrative to cut through moments of stark isolation. As author Anaïs Nin once wrote, "Stories are the only enchantment possible, for when we begin to see our suffering as a story, we are saved."

Looking at art to connect, reading to find a distinct voice—one that cuts through the darkness and seems to know your name—is not unlike a ramble down an imagined road, dust-filled, leaves crunching beneath your feet; when something unexpected draws your eye—a glint through the branches off to one side. A window perhaps? Or maybe a silver doorknob? You step off the road to explore this new thought. Sometimes it's nothing more than a flattened soda can. But sometimes that glimmer, that reflection, sets you on a new road.

In these pages, you will find a community of writers and artists. They are here to share a moment—through word, line, color, anything in their artists' toolboxes they can throw at you—hoping you'll make the catch and maybe even lob it back.

Though it may not be obvious, reading is a creative act. If you view what has been shared as a dialogue, then a response is required. You read. You write in response to what you read. And then you read some more. The same is true with visual art. You create in response to what has been created. Poetry begets poetry. Art begets art. If you aren't going to engage with the person speaking to you through line or image, then you may as well bounce a tennis ball against a wall.

Books, art—these are an invitation to engage. There is something divine in the physical act of translating ideas—ideas of love, fear, humanity—to fingertips to something that can be held and further shaped by someone else. The act itself is what satisfies, not the completed product. That is the beauty of the words and images on these pages. They were only sitting here stagnant until you came along to revive them. Thank you for sharing this moment. Our hope is you will now, in turn, add your thread to the narrative. Whether you write, create art, or simply read; engage.

Here, catch.

Bethanie Humphreys

Editor-In-Chief

Literature

Eleven

Bethanie Humphreys

1. One cloned
2. The edge of a bamboo forest
3. The result of careless shaving
4. A gymnast's Olympic dream
5. The "yuh" sound in Spanish
6. A fish-eye view of a New England ice skater
7. A broken ladder
8. September 10, 2001
9. A good relationship
10. A bad relationship (all relationships, really)
11. Vertical blinds after the hurricane
12. The road not taken
13. Pause
14. A pair of neutered exclamation points
15. Parentheses with the gay prayed out of them
16. An *H* on the diet pill from hell
17. An anorexic's dream thighs
18. My two front teeth, space and all
19. An unfortunate bottle rocket incident
20. The missing fingers
21. The death of the landline
22. A book, naked of pages

The Bitch

Eric Orosco

On the first Thursday of December, August Lambert watched her son's beagle propel upward into the sky. She watched from the southwest window of her living room while tasting her second glass of Lodi-grown pinot noir. From her vantage point, she could see the even green of her lawn, the blossoming birds of paradise edging the perimeter of her backyard fence, and the thin trunk of her young orange tree. What she couldn't see was the white, black, and brown fur of the beagle that had been barking nonstop.

Forgetting about the glass of wine in her hand, she leaned closer to the pane of glass and looked down into the backyard, taking note of the half-dug holes in and alongside her husband's garden and the litter of dog toys discarded in various moments of boredom. She looked up and took in the sky, its clouds floating above in amber, orange, purple, and red, all mixing together like a child's paint set. There appeared to be no disturbance in the sky, but she changed her vantage point to confirm, moving from the window to the sliding glass door.

A small dot, perhaps a recently detached balloon, rose into a billowing cloud of orange.

Resting one hand against the smooth metal handle of the door, the other pushing the thin glass of wine against her lips, she closed her eyes for a period of five seconds and inhaled. Blackberries. Cherries. Parting her lips, she tipped the glass gradually and allowed the liquid to trickle against the tip of her tongue, tart dissolving into a reminiscent sweet, a flush of red building beneath her cheeks. Eyes open, August stepped through the door and onto the cedar deck.

A breeze had developed and she pulled her arms closer to her body. She glanced along the grass where the beagle had been a moment ago and then glanced back

up at the clouds. The small dot had vanished. The beagle was gone.

"Shit." She exhaled, bending at the knees to grab a small, red rubber ball that rested on the deck. She took a guess at where the dog had been and tossed the ball toward that very spot, a few drops of pinot noir arcing out of the glass and staining the cedar. The ball sailed normally until it reached a certain point in the air above the grass, then, without a gradual transition, it launched vertically toward the very clouds she had just been looking at. "Shit."

The clock above the stove read 5:31. California Youth Basketball ended at 7:00 p.m., and the drive from the youth recreation center took twenty minutes tops if the traffic was agreeable, though as of late, her husband had taken even more time than usual. August set her glass of wine down on the marble counter next to the stove and leaned against the double door fridge, using a free hand to push the magnetic letters of the alphabet around in slow circles. Her hand mimicked the circles the beagle had made before its ascent into the clouds.

The dog had been sniffing the ground and barking in a way that caught August's attention after she poured her second glass of wine. She had watched the dog make three complete circles before it moved onto that specific patch of grass and launched upward. It had yelped in pain, but the yelp had also gone upward, the way a scream moves when a roller coaster zooms past and ascends into another loop.

She stopped her hand's circular motion and rested the tips of her fingers along the edge of a bulky, curved letter.

The bitch was gone.

Something had occurred in that single spot of grass and August wondered how long it could have been like that. Her husband had mowed the backyard three days prior and had not been launched upward, putting the timeline of appearance sometime between then, that sunny Saturday morning, to now, this sherbet skyline evening.

She imagined what it would have looked like if the lawnmower had run across the now deadly patch of grass—her, standing at the southwest window with lemonade in hand, watching Mr. Lambert mow in those salmon Bermudas from J. Crew—while the bitch barked and scratched at the sliding glass door. He'd look up at her and smile, loose cigarette dangling from the corner of his mouth. She'd stay still, watching him, the glare of the sun casting reflections on the window from his direction. That cigarette would tumble out of his mouth as the mower shot up into the air, one of his Sperry boat shoes being knocked off as he shot up as well, hands still gripping the mower with both instinct and panic, the scream of the roller coaster darting upward toward oblivion.

A knock at the door brought her out of the evening dream. Having startled, she knocked several of the magnetic letters to the floor and turned to the window in the living room. Since the initial incident, the natural lighting had diminished into a faint evening glow that was overpowered by the orange streetlights alongside her house. The clock jumped to 6:03, and as she watched the minute change to 6:04, another series of knocks began on her door. August glanced over her shoulder at the southwest-facing window before going to the front door.

Through the peephole, August caught sight of permed red curls and remembered it was her night to do a patrol for Neighborhood Watch. Kathy Harris stood in the small circle of the peephole, adjusting her high-waisted jeans and holiday sweater.

"Hello Kathy," August said after opening the front door and stepping out onto the porch. She caught a whiff of Elizabeth Taylor's White Diamonds perfume mixed with the scents of a California winter. Kathy smiled without showing teeth, her dimples manifesting beneath a layer of rose blush.

"August," Kathy said, "thought you weren't going to show."

As they stepped off the front porch in unison, Kathy switched on the official Neighborhood Watch flashlight and swept its beam along the garage and side gate. The focused light caught the fading outline of a basketball

backboard above the metal garage door, hesitated for a second on this remnant, then continued as though it had not noticed a single thing.

"Didn't hear your dog bark when I knocked," Kathy said as she rummaged through the fanny pack attached to her waist. She pulled out a small pocket notepad and pen and handed the bundle to August.

"The dog is gone." August flipped open to a new page and wrote down the current date.

"Christ. Guess the mister is finally coming to his senses. Wasn't right keeping the damned thing, let alone that damned job as basketball coach. Wrapping yourself up in the past does no good, I can tell you that much. You mourn. You move on. And that's all there is to it." Across the street, a couple wearing highlighter-yellow sweaters jogged in unison. "Have you two thought about moving? Getting out of that house would do wonders for both of you." The joggers were at the end of the street now, the man jogging in place while the woman stretched her left calf against a streetlamp. "We'd hate losing you, especially since you always chair our big Street Safety Gala, but we'd understand, August. We'd understand if you moved."

"I'm sure you would, Kathy." August took down the description of the joggers and their approximate position at 6:15 p.m.

"There are plenty of us to take on the responsibilities. I've been your co-chair for years, August. Even if you just wanted to take a break this time around, I'd be more than happy to chair the committee myself."

They paused a moment as Kathy bent down to tie the lace of her sneaker that had come undone. August heard the roar of a roller coaster from far away. Distant, but growing closer. Kathy's red lips were moving, but August was focused on the roar that sounded as though it were now inches away from her ears.

Standing above Kathy, she imagined gravity reversing below that untied sneaker and the flailing of Kathy as she shot up into the darkening sky. August looked up and imagined seeing the bright red of those permed

curls disappear into the black, the sound of her screams and the roller coaster fading off into the oblivion above.

At 7:00 p.m., August said goodnight to Kathy and walked back up the driveway and into her empty house. It was still and quiet, but the faint smell of a dog lingered in the air. August wondered how long it would be before the bitch's scent dissolved into nothing. Would she smell her weeks from now when walking across the living room carpet? Would she be reminded of the bitch in the dead of the night when her ears picked up on a phantom yapping? The dead linger in many ways. August tried to prepare herself for what was to come.

She made her way to the kitchen where her wineglass rested, holding a centimeter or so of liquid. It had to have been some reversal of gravity that caused the bitch to shoot up into the air, or at least that seemed the most probable to August. Her thoughts were wrapped up in ideas of gravity and space and clouds until the crunching of cheap plastic stopped her progress. She raised her foot and saw the splintered yellow carcass of the letter B.

The letters were another of the items Mr. Lambert had decided to leave in the house. She caught glimpses of the other plastic letters poking out from under the refrigerator, the way a child's feet appear when he hides himself under a bed he can't quite fit under. August used the front of her shoe to kick the letters farther back under the refrigerator. Her thoughts returned to her husband. He'd cry when he got home and saw that the bitch was gone. He'd cry and prostrate himself in a pile of the bitch's toys.

August would watch him do this, his tears dripping down onto slippery, shitty rubber. She'd point to the spot the dog had last been, and he'd collapse to his knees at the very edge of the antigravity, screaming at the clouds, begging for the bitch's return.

At some point in the night, she'd leave him to go take a shower. Sliding off her clothes, she'd submerge herself in a running stream of warmth and wash her body with rosemary and sea salts. After washing, she'd stay beneath the showerhead for many more minutes, feeling the streams of water like a million miniature punches against her skin. Through the built-up steam, she'd step

out of the shower and onto the chilled tile of the bathroom floor, droplets of water coasting down, dewing the
fine hairs on her body until a few lone drops managed to
find themselves removed from the flesh and free-falling
onto the tile. Her husband would be on the edge of the
bed, looking up at her dripping body in the steam. He'd
want to see her cry. He'd demand it.

August grabbed her wineglass and leaned against the
marble counter, sipping to the image of her husband
and the lingering sensation of water on skin. She could
almost smell the faint scent of rosemary mixing with the
blackberries and cherries of her wine.

Something thudded on the cedar deck. She glanced
at the unlit backyard and downed the final bit of pinot
noir. She walked toward the sliding door. The night was
dark and she could only see her reflection growing larger
in the glass.

She flipped the switch, and a dull light came on,
illuminating the deck and parts of the grass, the edges
of the backyard still wrapped in darkness. Her eyes
scanned the scene until she saw the red rubber ball resting in the grass. She inhaled sharply as oblivion returned
what it had taken.

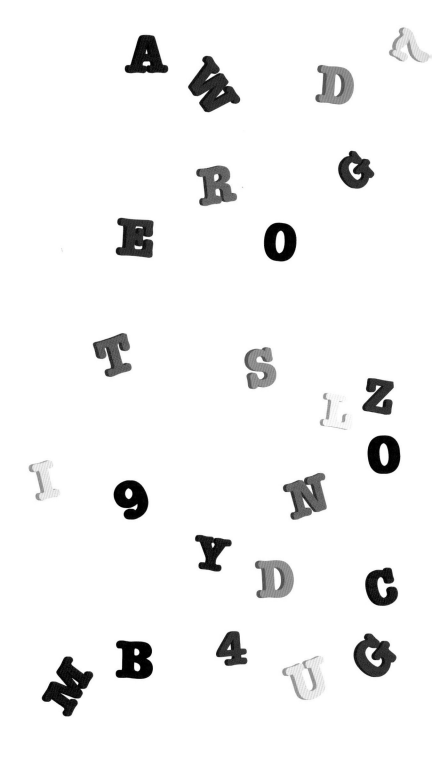

Window Rain

Carlitta Cole-Kelly

Ah, California rain—for me it is a purposeful tranquility, peaceful, and much needed, relieving the drought of both land and spirit. With an early morning mist, it dissipates into the ridges of my backyard's aged wooden fences, hushed down from satisfied blue-gray skies. Damp tree leaves fall sullenly from once thirsty branches to the ground below. Trickling along aluminum rooftop gutters to downspouts or puddles resting atop patio tables, western rain has a way of slowing everything d-o-w-n. The freshness in the air cast behind or the cozy atmosphere it creates inside a house can capture moments of clear reflection. Find a bed, better yet, one with a thick duvet, that's been left unmade. Slither underneath a warm comforter with an engrossing book, soft lighting from an old lamp, and try to fight off the sleep. Just try it.

This is new rain. It always is, unlike the Mississippi rain that once pounded onto our tin roof in Biloxi. It cascaded unapologetically along deep tin roof grooves down onto the edges of our wooden porch. The rain of those days was wet with childhood curiosity and things we imagined lurking alongside us as we danced in the fog or the smoky mist that trailed behind pesticide-spraying mosquito trucks. There, the summer rainstorms tried to outrun the sun daily, while the Devil's wife deep in Hell below was getting a beating because of it—so my grandmother said.

"Turn the lights and TV off. Let God do His work," she'd announce as thunder cracked or lightning streaked across an unforgiving afternoon sky. A naked light bulb once shining bright in its ceiling socket was quickly yanked by a string into submission. "Mama and Daddy Dewey," as I called them, could either sit in silence listening to the rain or chat easily. Daddy, whose eyes were green, was perfectly pale for a man of mixed race. He'd sit in his favorite worn-out wood slat chair, long lanky legs

crossed, sipping coffee from a blue and white speckled tin cup. Once again, the rain prevented him from watching his favorite character, Festus, on the TV show *Gunsmoke*. He and Mama would talk about who they had run into while handling business or working in town or about the family my grandmother worked for as a maid. Though her job was to cook and clean up after them, it bothered her that they had little gumption for doing more of it for themselves. The children were sometimes disrespectful to their parents, causing my grandmother to bite her tongue more often than she liked. Still, servitude had its limits, and she was known to tell them a thing or two if necessary. Stories about "The Lindseys" were always engaging.

But for me, watching rain fall outside the bedroom window was even better. Quarter-sized drops of rain splattered onto the window ledge outside my bedroom. Cohesive, little bubbles that eventually dissolved into a trickle fell down deep into the muddy ground below the willow tree, never to be seen again. Elsewhere, heavy raindrops would dance atop a rusty fishing toolbox or linger stubbornly at the tips of my grandparents' fishing poles, which leaned up against the house. The poles kept company with other luckless objects left outside before a swift downpour. Sheets, shirts, and cotton dresses were quickly snatched from thick-roped lines strung between two Y-shaped wooden posts in the backyard. Some clothing still had a wooden clothespin or two intact. In the front yard, underneath the porch, dogs and whatever else dared to hunker alongside them found shelter there from the rain.

Still, inside is where the real waiting began.

My grandparents' small, hunter green house withstood many regiments of rain, along with the storms and hurricanes they suckered into town. It sat at 512 Couevas Street,

about a mile from Keesler Air Force Base and only blocks from the beach. Fairly weatherproof, two additions had been proudly hand-built by my grandfather, a dedicated lumber-yard worker. Inside its four rooms during heavy rainstorms, buckets and small pots or pans were positioned in place over the linoleum floor, catching rainwater that intruded from a rusted hole in the tin roof. Daddy Dewey tackled each new hole as best he could but just hadn't gotten to others yet. Plap, plap, pling! as water hit heavy metal bottoms, then plunk! as each receptacle began to slowly fill up. Yet we were kept warm and comfy inside by handmade quilts and little, portable, ceramic space heaters, despite rambunctious drops of rain or cold drafts of air that somehow stole their way inside.

Some days of window rain I spent lying quietly on the bed reading a library book, interrupted only by thunder or a rumbling in the ground that signaled a fast approaching train passing through at the southern end of Couevas. There, the tracks lay just yards from Biloxi's Ice House. The train's whistle left me wondering where travelers had come from and where they might now be going. Other rainy days included playing with paper doll cutouts, covering each figure with a new dress and accessories. It mattered whether my scissors were sharp enough to cut new designs from magazine pages. It was equally important to prevent folds or tears in the paper. An only child living with her grandparents must learn to find fun, solitary, and entertaining things to do while waiting out the rain.

It wasn't until one day, decades later, when I found myself lying quietly in bed reading a book, that I rediscovered window rain. Snuggled underneath the covers, I had not only watched it fall, but I heard it progress to a heavier than usual pounding on the roof. It had arrived in a rare, swift, heavy downpour, while a train whistled somewhere in the distance.

Why hadn't I heard these sounds before now? Where had they been?

Somehow, I'd long since forgotten them both—the rains and trains—and how together they'd often kept a nine-year-old girl and her books and paper dolls company. I'd failed to recall the contentment that came from simple conversations with people who loved and protected you from the thunder,

lightning, and uninvited rainstorms. I'd forgotten about a community of people who seldom feared hurricanes like Katrina, while respecting those like Camille. Whether folks sheltered in place in their homes or moved to safer ground seemed to have no rhyme or reason at all. They just did or didn't, then got on with whatever challenges the storm left behind.

Today, the Mississippi Gulf Coast welcomes its tourists. It is illuminated with restaurants, hotels, and neon casino lights from tall buildings. But our family loves remembering the little house on Couevas Street and all that she has weathered. We treasure her days ahead. The address has long since been renumbered and the hull rebuilt with red brick, courtesy of the city.

But the rain still comes. It always will.

Somehow in the years after leaving Biloxi, I'd overlooked how it feels to live with rain, the kind that drops down from thick clouds. I'd learned to live without it, that is, until a drizzle and faint train whistle out west reminded me what I'd been missing for far too long.

I'd simply forgotten how to appreciate rain, its coming and its going.

Ah, the rains of two coasts, one sorely missed in the summertime of the South and the other welcomed in spring or found wandering aimlessly through wintry days out West. Perhaps it isn't only the window rain itself that I miss now, but rather the clarity and comfort of being content inside, and out of the rain that really waters my soul. Or just maybe, remembering it patiently through the window of a child's eyes is now what I look forward to hearing, seeing, and feeling even more.

Bareback

Velvet Sharon McKenzie

My father broke horses
cleared wombs
pulled calves

Never-ending breeds to birch
tied to the tailgate of a '57 Chevy
bit busted
they bucked him from their saddle
not me
not my mother

Mares
shoved under
stallions
their hooves carved his lover's name
in mounds of shit

While mother shoveled stalls
a hundred times
never clean
enough

They'd drop
bile, blood, and grass
on her roses
until they grew, tall
robust
mad blooms

Pinkyellowpurplewhite
her American garden
the triumph of suburbia
drew wind
and blew
the scent of foreign women
into our neighbor's yard

Sylvia's Scissors

Velvet Sharon McKenzie

Red hands rummage
your train-cased thoughts
electrocutions, pill drawers, and pantyhose
until I pull you to sad pieces
regret
carving up your home-sewn dress
cigarette burns on final drafts
severing blond starlet hair
that falls like brass
curls cut
from mother's Christmas angel, when
I learned
some things cannot grow back

only up

I grew
to watch you
paint your cottage
with raw meat
each board a rib of Adam
you'd never steal

Housewives winked from oven
windows
Your ego poured in bourbon
broke glass
crushed milk and ribbons
ice buckets and bramble bread

I try to meet you
on canvas or courtyard
strike
through
~~what always was~~
in the red
~~the red~~
the bone
the glue
that stuck the wings
from the father's bees that kept you
brushed thick
ash-ink and honey
painting mirrors
until the piss was shook
from every word

The perfect edge
of scissors
that never cut
the sting

14 Dead Dogs

Caitlin Pegar

1.
I was named Britney when I was born.
My mom's favorite cocker spaniel died three months beforehand.
The dog's name was Britney.

2.
Scruff died of old age when I was two.
He lay down in a cardboard box, swaddled in blankets, only his head poking out, and died.
My earliest memory is of a dog's head with its eyes so open they're bulging out and a mouth stretched to its limits in its final breath.

3.
Tiny was hit by a truck as a puppy.
My mom had told me people go to Heaven when they die.
Looking at the two halves of Tiny, I asked if he would go to Heaven.
She said no.

4.
One year later, Killer had a brain tumor.
Mom decided that dogs do, in fact, go to doggie Heaven.
I asked if I could go to doggie Heaven instead of regular Heaven.
She said no.

5.
Scooby was the only one of our dogs to ever get rabies. We found that out when he bit me.
Luckily I didn't contract it, but Scooby had to be put to sleep.
I still never received any vaccinations, but the dogs did.

6.

We moved to the country when I was thirteen and bought a few sheep, a flock of chickens, a hog, and a sow.

Prince usually herded the sheep.

He was not supposed to try to herd the pigs.

7.

I repeatedly told my mother not to let her new boyfriend name the new pug "Lucky."

Only bad things could come of it, though I changed my mind at the end.

Because finally succumbing after being crushed by the garage door for the fifth time within a month had nothing to do with luck.

8.

Moscow was put down by animal control after she was discovered living in our dorm.

A crowd gathered to watch after the labrador ripped apart the tendons in my RA's leg.

My roommate bawled for hours, clutching my arm. I didn't really cry over her dog, but because I had to move on a budget of 46 bucks.

9.

Near the end of their lives, Mother willed that Duchess's ashes be added to her own, because Heaven is all-inclusive now.

10.

My husband and I decided to get a dog before having a child, which was silly, because while growing up, I had much better luck babysitting neighborhood kids than watching my mother's dogs.

He named the pointer Einstein.

I told him that was a terrible idea.

Einstein was hit by lightning, which was tragic, but all I could think of was comparing him to Lucky.

11.

My neighbor's mutt, Celery, liked to bark through the chain link fence at our dog, Loki, who was just as eager to bark back.

Celery grabbed Loki's muzzle and pulled it through the chain, ripping off a good amount of skin.

We didn't hear the commotion until the fence was down and there was only one throat between the two of them.

12.

I was terribly happy when Celery had to be put down too.

13.

Sassafrass had seven toes on each paw, apparently a result of inbreeding. Still, great dog, well-trained, very smart. She taught herself to climb ladders.

She taught herself to climb ladders.

Don't get smart dogs.

14.

Pippi knocked over Edith's urn. As they lay on the ground, I tried to see if I could separate Edith's ashes from Duchess's, but Pippi was content to lick them both.

I stopped her from eating them, but I gave up trying to put my mother and her dog back into the urn.

I dug out an old necklace and a matching dog collar, and just put those in instead.

Afterward, I gave Pippi her insulin shot and waited for another day.

Lady Madonna Folds

Bethanie Humphreys

She cleaned the garage.

It hadn't been cleaned once in the two years they'd lived in the mud-brown duplex on Grayson Road. They'd moved from a two-bedroom apartment after throwing their stuff into refried bean, canned peach, and pickle boxes markered over with Living Room, Kitchen, Boys Room. They moved over a weekend and hadn't had time to unpack much beyond the cereal bowls, spoons, and underwear before going back to work and school on Monday. Or since.

She remembered how excited she'd been to finally have her own washer and dryer. Three boys under seven makes a washing machine as much of a luxury as matching gym socks.

She cleaned the garage so her car would fit. Ten garbage bags of crap taken to Goodwill, high chair and bouncer to the neighbors across the street with an ever-swelling flock of kids, empty boxes flattened and shoved in a corner, and done. It had been put off for so long, yet it took less than two hours to finish.

Even nearly empty, the garage still looked dirty. She retrieved the broom and dustpan that were buried beneath a drooping stack of fallen towels in the linen closet. She swept the litter of empty webs, gray lint tumbleweeds, and drywall crumbling along the walls like irregular hunks of dehydrated marshmallow. The bedraggled broom left streaks of white dust across the cement floor like a drunken Zen garden. She gave up, trashing the broom along with the contents of the dustpan. The garage now smelled of sidewalk chalk, almost pleasant compared to the usual aroma of work and play-torn clothes.

Earlier that morning:

"Boys, get your shoes on. Time to go." She felt around her in purse for her keys.

"Mom, where's my sweatshirt?" Vincent asked, slipping his tennis shoes on without tying them.

"Which one?"

"The dead racecar driver one."

"Um, under the chair." She finally fished out her keys. "Jackson, TV off. Shoes now!"

Toby wound himself around her leg. "Mama, is it a stay-home day?"

"No, honey it's Wednesday." She bent and helped him tie his shoes.

Vincent grabbed his backpack, shouted, "Bus is leaving!" and slammed the front door behind him. Toby wailed, tried to go after him, but his hands kept slipping on the knob.

"He can't leave without us honey. I have the keys." She opened the door for him and he tore down the sidewalk after his brother.

She turned off the lights in the back bedrooms. No sign of Jackson in the house, so she locked the front door. As she walked around the car to buckle Toby into his booster seat, she only saw two heads. "Where's Jackson?"

she asked them. They both shrugged. She slammed Toby's door, ran back up the walk, and unlocked the front door, yanking it open. "Jackson, we're late!"

Silence.

"Jackson!" She heard a chair scrape the linoleum in the kitchen. He was kneeling behind the kitchen table, just like his daddy had the last two nights. Sick of the droppings and holes chewed into their cereal boxes, he had set out a peanut butter-baited mousetrap in the corner behind the table, much to the delight of Vince and Toby. Jackson had stayed in his room, not wanting them to make fun of his urge to protect the small intrusive creature.

"Jackson, get your ass into the car. Now."

He was using a pretzel stick to try and get the trap to snap, but it wasn't working. He wouldn't look up at her. "I thought maybe if we caught it without hurting it, it could live in Frankie's cage."

He looked so forlorn, she gritted her teeth to keep from yelling. "It wouldn't work honey. They'd probably just kill each other."

He didn't say anything. She looked at the clock, and yanked him to his feet. "Don't tell Vince and Toby," he pled.

"You're late," she said and pushed him a little too hard out the door. He tripped on the threshold and started to cry. She locked the front door and stepped around him to the car.

Once her car was parked in the garage, she thought to look for the garden hose, but remembered their neighbor's dog had chewed through it just as the autumn cold came creeping in to kill off what few scraggled patches of grass were spared by the August sun. There didn't seem to be any point in replacing the hose then. But now? The garage was small. A few hours should be enough.

Before going inside, she shoveled the load of darks into the dryer and tossed the pile of towels and a stray sock into the washer. These two loads were the last. She pushed the button and stood to watch the garage door unscroll, replacing dead trees and houses with contrived darkness.

Back in the kitchen, continuing down her mental checklist—she emptied the dishwasher, stacked mismatched plates and bowls on the yellowed and curling shelf paper, angled in chipped coffee mugs with the last of the sippy cups, wiped down the kitchen counters. She went to get the broom, but remembered she had thrown it away. She couldn't remember the last time the floor was mopped. When Toby began to crawl, she'd been so tempted to hire a cleaning service, even called one out to give an estimate, knowing they couldn't afford it.

Following the trail out of the kitchen, she picked up random toys, tennis shoes, cups, and bowls scattered in the living room and strewn like hopscotch down the hall. She often yelled at the boys to pick up after themselves, not that it helped much. She stood in the dim hall for a moment with an armful of toys. Her plan was to pick up in the boys' rooms too, the whole house, but she couldn't bear to go in. Vince's walls covered in monster truck posters, the floor littered with papers from school, sports equipment, a crumbling clay volcano that was last year's science project. Jackson and Toby's room was a mishmash of shoes, toys, and a maze they made

18

for the hamster out of a giant cardboard box.

Instead she threw the toys into the closet, closed their doors, grabbed the flannel blanket from her bed, and folded herself up on the couch. It felt better not to move. Maybe not better, just familiar.

She had called in sick the last three days. Her mother-in-law insisted on picking up the boys every afternoon, even when she wasn't sick, so all she had to do was drop them off at school and daycare in the morning and then spend the rest of the day on the couch.

Watching *Miller's Crossing* over and over, wearing the same sweats, same dark knot of hair on her nape. She ate the same instant oatmeal and ramen noodle soup. The only thing that had changed recently, in what felt like years, was the pattern on her tissue box. A minor cold had given her an excuse to not work so hard the last few days at pretending to be okay.

She used to eat up free days. Even sick, she could still balance the checkbook, do some laundry, and relish reading more than a paragraph at a time without interruption. It used to help.

Her battered box of journals from the garage, even the journal in her underwear drawer, she'd thrown them all away. There was a distant, muffled clang of alarm. She could hear it through her haze, but couldn't stop the sinking. The only thing left on her mental list was whether to leave a note.

She should leave a note . . . the kids. Her husband. This would become the most memorable thing she ever wrote. They would dig into each word, each syllable, deconstruct the syntax and context and squeeze every drop of meaning they could from every single speck and wrinkle and comma. And it would never be enough. Did she really want them to read something she wrote when she had nothing to say? When there was no good explanation?

The laundry buzzer sounded. Slowly she rolled over, pushed up from the coffee table, let the blanket trail off and puddle behind her on the living room floor. The garage still smelled of wet towels and chalk. The washer and dryer looked strangely white and small without their usual accompanying piles. She pulled the warm darks into her yellow laundry basket, and wrestled the wet towels into the dryer. Last load.

She carried the heavy basket down the unlit hall toward her room. Her mother-in-law would move in. The woman was always hinting at it, wanting to help more with the kids. The offers were well intentioned, but only served as another reminder of her endless failures as a mother, a list that wagged like a finger in her face from every corner of the house.

The heater kicked on, blowing the smell of burnt hair from the vents. Balancing the basket on her hip, she flipped the thermostat off. The bill was too high last month. She overturned the clothes onto her unmade bed and set the basket on the floor.

She picked up a sweatshirt from the top of the pile. It crackled with static electricity, and the shock of warmth on her cold hands almost made her drop it. She held it against her cheek. A tiny moan escaped. Dipping forward into the pile, she slid onto the bed and scooped the clothes out from under and pulled them over herself, curling into a ball. So warm. Warmer than she had been in months. Her throat caught. She started to cry, but it was just the ground swell.

There was no one she could talk to. Her mother would just tell her again how lucky she was to have married a man that didn't drink a six-pack for breakfast like her dear old dad, wherever that deadbeat was. Her husband

was a good man, almost as buried as she was, yet he somehow managed to keep his head above ground. She hated her friends. Not really. She was just weary of having to explain yet again why even though she loathed her job at the call center she couldn't leave because they were so flexible whenever her kids were sick, had dentist appointments, and so on. And worse, if she made much more, they would no longer qualify for daycare assistance. And if they didn't get daycare assistance, she couldn't work. And they couldn't afford for her not to work.

She used to dream of being a writer, a stay-at-home mom tapping away at the keyboard while the kids were napping or in school. What sort of a tax-bracket do you have to be in for one person to support a family of five now? Health insurance, housing, food, clothes, transportation—it just seemed impossible. She never felt like writing anymore anyway.

As the last bit of warmth was sucked out of her pile by the frigid house, she crawled out and picked up a tiny pair of blue jeans, Toby's. At least the kids were doing okay for the most part. When she wasn't yelling at them, that is. She folded a little red and white striped polo and layered it on top of the jeans. They would be okay. Eventually.

Three black sweatshirts covered in skulls and racecars in Vince's stack. He was finally learning to read, after so much struggling the last two years. Homework sessions were a nightmare. Work, then home, dinner, then a scant half an hour till bedtime when everyone was already exhausted, and that's all the time they had. She knew his trouble with reading was her fault. There was never time to read with him by the time all the workbook pages were done.

She started another stack for Jackson's clothes—all brown or blue, animals and fish. Jackson had been absolutely petrified of starting kindergarten after seeing Vincent's hell. She wished for the time and patience to homeschool like some of her friends did but knew she would never have enough of either. At least in some ways they were better off in public school.

The clothes were half folded, but she was thirsty. After shuffling into the kitchen for some water, her hand froze at the cupboard door. She thought she heard a faint scratching sound by the kitchen table. It couldn't be. In the middle of the day? She stepped up on a chair, holding onto the back with both hands, looked down, and stifled a scream. Blood was smeared all over the floor, and a small gray mouse dangled awkwardly from one side of the trap. It wasn't moving. Was it dead? It must have been gnawing at its hind leg, dragging the trap around in circles like a monstrous wooden shoe. Shit.

She got down and grabbed her kitchen gloves and a trash bag from under the sink. Moving the chair out of the way, she knelt, but couldn't bring herself to pick it up, even with gloves. Grabbing a grubby towel from the closet, she laid it over the mouse, trap and all. Nothing happened. *Please be dead.* Tucking the sides underneath, she shoved it quickly into the garbage bag and left it on the floor as she stood up. She waited. Not a rustle. She sprayed bleach on the tired linoleum and wiped up the blood with paper towels, keeping her head turned away as much as possible.

She took the bag to the trash bin outside, holding it out in front of her as if it already smelled. After dropping the bag in, she stood holding the lid open for a moment, staring blankly. She peeled off the kitchen gloves and threw those in too. Back inside, she washed her hands. Twice.

She wandered back down the hall to the garage to check the laundry. The buzzer was about to go off, but the

towels were still damp. She added more time, then stood for a moment listening to the whir and tumble. Her little red car looked abstract in the enclosed space. It was so dirty it was almost orange. One of the boys had drawn sad faces in jail in the dust on the back windows. She actually hated bright colors, but chose red because of its visibility—if people can see you, they are less likely to hit you. The irony of a car chosen for safety ultimately becoming her method of escape was not lost on her. But the thought was not welcome either. It would work without a hose, wouldn't it?

Pressing her fingers into her eyes, she went back into the house to lie down, but the laundry was still on the bed. She sighed, and picked up a small pair of sweatpants. Toby's. He seemed to like preschool, came home with all kinds of tissue paper ghosts, handprint turkeys, green and orange paint down these pants. Why on earth don't they use washable paint with four-year-olds? She dropped the stained pants back into the basket to rewash later, picked up a t-shirt and started to fold it, then stopped.

She looked down at the stained pants lying askew in the basket. She hadn't planned to do any more laundry, ever again. She slowly unfolded the shirt she had just picked up, brown with black bears on the front, and brought it to her face. Jackson's. Oh God. She could never tell him about the mouse. The dull ache rooted in her chest for so many months suddenly spiked and flowered out into her limbs in painful spasms. Her knees started to give. The three stacks of clothes slanted up in a steady grade of hills into mountain peaks across her bed, Toby's small stack, Jackson's bigger, Vince's falling over. How could she ever set it right?

Dropping to her knees beside the bed, still clutching Jackson's shirt, her face tight, jaw locked open, no sound. How could she? Dear God, how could she? She pressed the shirt against her mouth, against the storm.

The laundry buzzer sounded.

On autopilot, she stiffly pulled herself up from the floor and headed for the garage. Her car waited, with its dust and Cheerios and broken crayons and crumpled napkins. There had to be another way to get through, get past this, but how? There wasn't much that could be changed in her day-to-day routine, but that didn't mean she was stuck forever in the same seasonless inertia. Did it?

She turned, tracing her hands along the walls toward the living room, waiting for the stumble. As she passed Jackson and Toby's room, she could hear Frankie spinning noisily in his wheel. He seemed pretty happy not getting anywhere. She found her phone on the coffee table and held it to her chest for a moment. The sky outside the living room window was just as flat and mind-numbingly gray as it had been for days. She opened her phone and pressed two for her mother-in-law. Not bothering with any of the usual niceties, "Yeah, it's me. I'll pick up the boys today."

Not half a beat later, "Positive."

Peanut Butter & Jelly Days

Bethanie Humphreys

Jenny picked up a twig and squished an ant with it. "Come on," she said to Mike and started down the trail without looking to see if he followed.

Mike pushed off the rock and grabbed his pack, looking back the way they'd come. Jenny's jaw tightened when she caught his backward glance. "Quit worrying about the stupid dog. She's fine." He'd brought home a puppy the week after she'd miscarried. The squirmy thing was worse than cut flowers. She couldn't throw it in the green waste like sunshiny daisies after a week of the petals curling into themselves.

He was giving his best hangdog face, but she didn't look back. "I was just thinking we should've brought some PB&Js like we used to. You know, eat on the trail."

"We can afford to eat out every once in a while now." She kept moving, quickening her pace.

"I know," he said. "More of a sentimental thing."

But she didn't hear the last part. Peanut butter and jelly, character lunchboxes, a thermos of tepid milk. She pictured him with an infant carrier strapped to his chest—and was secretly glad it would never fill the space between them.

Irene

Blake Steele

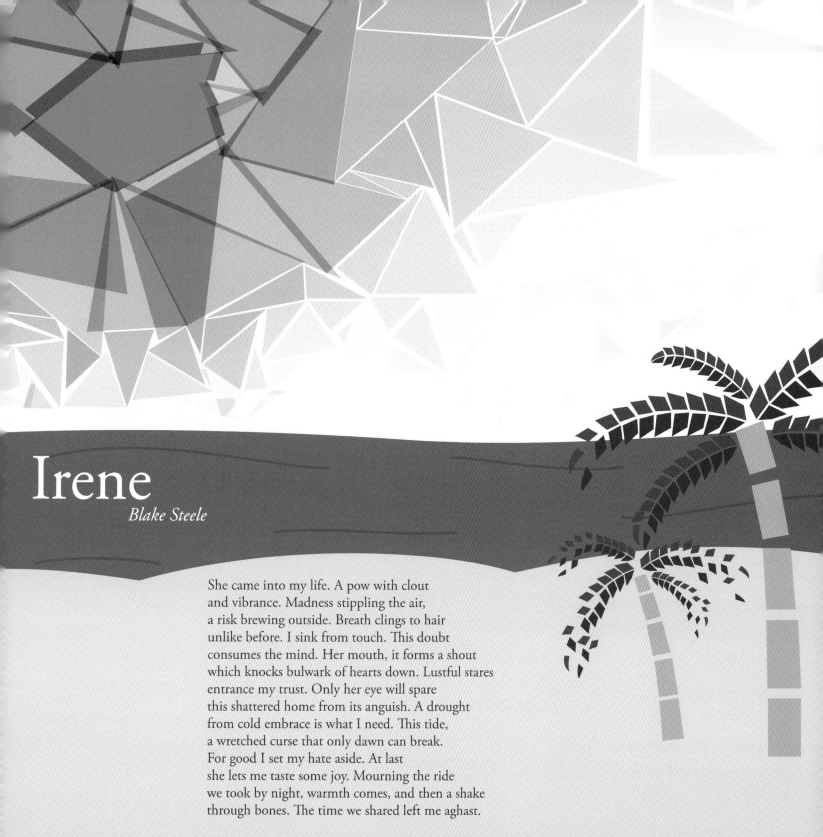

She came into my life. A pow with clout
and vibrance. Madness stippling the air,
a risk brewing outside. Breath clings to hair
unlike before. I sink from touch. This doubt
consumes the mind. Her mouth, it forms a shout
which knocks bulwark of hearts down. Lustful stares
entrance my trust. Only her eye will spare
this shattered home from its anguish. A drought
from cold embrace is what I need. This tide,
a wretched curse that only dawn can break.
For good I set my hate aside. At last
she lets me taste some joy. Mourning the ride
we took by night, warmth comes, and then a shake
through bones. The time we shared left me aghast.

The Procrastinator's Pantoum

Austin Ice

Ugh, why didn't my alarm go off
Where are my pants
It's too hot for school today
Keys—keys—where are they

Where are my pants
I'll just have to grab some toast
Keys—keys—where are they
I can't be late for class AGAIN

I'll just have to grab some toast
. . . I just put Preparation H on my toothbrush
I can't be late for class AGAIN
Wait; where's my toothpaste then

. . . I just put Preparation H on my toothbrush
Where did I put my friggin' books
Wait; where's my toothpaste then
And I didn't charge my phone

Where did I put my friggin' books
Phew, is that my socks
And I didn't charge my phone
Oh shit; the paper

Phew, is that my socks
Please, please—no pop quiz today
Oh shit; the paper
Doesn't matter, it'll have to work

Please, please—no pop quiz today
What happened to all my gas
Doesn't matter, it'll have to work
You know what, screw this

What happened to all my gas
Ugh, why didn't my alarm go off
You know what, screw this
It's too hot for school today

Speech to the Saginaw County Rotarians

Rachel Gardner

Salve and hello to the friends, family, and partners of the Saginaw County Rotary Club. You might know me as that gray skeleton that played Santa the year Jeff Treadwell was sick, but I'm actually the emcee for tonight.

pause for applause

I'm assuming you're all here for Marge's mold salad, so allow me to give you directions to the buffet line in order to maximize the background noise of chewing during my speech.

pause for laughter

I think we've all met Herb Stanfield one way or another, usually by the bar.

brief pause for laughter

But most of us, I'm sure, know Herb from his duties as treasurer, fundraiser, and all-around man on the spot for the past thirty years.

pause for obligatory family hooting

Herb was one of the founding fathers of the Saginaw Club, and his level of dedication can only rate the highest of honors: a cheap alloy pocket watch.

ponder waistband of underwear creeping up your midsection

I'm sure I don't need to tell anyone here about his level of dedication, the hours he put in, the sweat he sacrificed, the lawyers he punched—

smile coyly at visiting district attorney

—and the longnecks he knocked back. Our Herb is quite a drinker, isn't he, folks? But enough about Lake Watahanoe.

pause for feigned laughter

I'm sure we've all heard the phrase, 'It's not what you know, it's who you know,' and folks, I can bet right now that not a one of you in this room hasn't felt Herb's hand on your back . . . or unmentionables.

cough, as if you're fooling anyone

Really, I guess you can't count a body in this room that hasn't helped Herb in some way; something about him just brings out this county's generosity of spirit. Cash, casseroles, a friendly ear when he came under fire in '86. Folks weren't about to let a few schoolgirls put our own local Plautus on the spot. I'm sure we all remember the kerfuffle—no need to name names, on account of the injunction—oh, there I go using those ten-dollar words of mine.

slap wrist

But I'm sure we'd all say that Herb has also been pivotal for much of the policy change in the Rotary Club itself. I'm not sure if any of you were there for the day we allowed the ladies in as members. All five minutes of it.

pause to reflect on life's missed opportunities; stop halfway or you'll be here all night

You know, I near fell over from shock when they gave me this job. I really do have to apologize for this. Guess I'm not much of a public speaker. Thing is, we couldn't very well have Herb getting up here and trumpeting his own accomplishments, could we? Then what the heck would separate today from the other 364 days of the year?

pretend to reach for water to create feedback squeal when your hand hits the mic cord

take advantage of momentary distraction to extract your underwear from crack canyon

I guess you could say Herb's shaped us all like a rock shapes the crotch of a tree it's lodged in. What you have in Herb is the proverbial sidehill gouger; you either move aside or starve 'cause he sure as heckfire ain't gonna move. He's the only man I've ever seen give a criminal deposition from a rocking chair. And Lord knows we're all a lot more careful with our daughters than we were in '85. Well . . . those of us that have 'em. Only in Saginaw could a man like Herb become a fixture, I tell you. Any other town would've run him out, or at least given him a government job. You know, I once applied for treasurer. Yeah. But they said Herb's gotta have it. He's got kids to feed. Some of them his, anyway.

nod at relatives sitting stone-faced through the speech

But enough of me running my jaw. I'll get back to the blandishments—there you go, another ten-dollar word of mine—and let you folks gather your coats. I know you're all itchin' to hit the road, or the john after Marge's mold salad. They told me to fill twenty-five minutes, and by God and His tiny little cherubim I will, even if that means I have to say, 'The quick brown fox jumped over the lazy dog,' seventeen times in succession. That's what they'll say about me, 'He filled up twenty-five minutes.' Put it on my tombstone, eat the flowers, and burn the hymnals.

stare at the water as if that alone will transmogrify it into alcohol

You know . . . the thing they never tell you when you get your degree is what you'll be using it for. I never thought I'd be up in front of all of you, talking about someone like Herb. I was never much for public speaking, just never got the opportunity, I guess. But Jeff, he tells me there isn't anyone else to do it. And I have to wonder, in this fine flock of countrymen we have here tonight, there's not a one of you who could have come up here and done this for me?

pause and gaze soul-searchingly out into the sea of faces

Let's face it, we're not honoring a man tonight, we're honoring an idea. An idea that clings to us, no matter how hard we try to dislodge its fingers from our throat. Herb is a small man for a small town, and he is all we deserve.

raise glass

To Herb, to life. *Morituri te salutant.*

pause for crippling silence

go home and drink yourself stupid

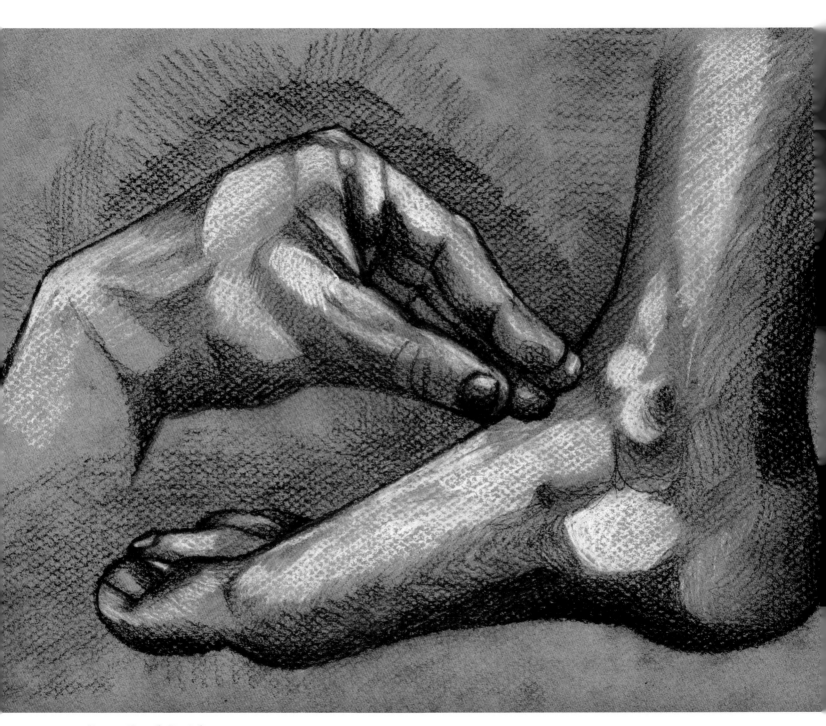

Liam Byrd-Smith
Hand + Foot Study
Charcoal on Gray Paper
9x12 Inches

Skin Deep

Caitlin Pegar

I.

At night I lay alone
watching the wrinkles of my wrists
touch fingertips one atop another
trying to feel through the nail

Bathing the aged paper of her
gentle where she cannot be
wedged between wrinkles
I find hints, stories, her
littered scars lost from memory
I find parties and books, weddings
work, the scar that bore my brothers
Sponging between her folds
soaking up what's left
of all the things she told me
before I learned to listen

II.

At night I lay alone
pondering the pores of my breasts
touch fingertips together
trying to feel two places at once

Air moves across my cheek
cotton slides beneath my back
my hand near hers
I kick the wool off our legs
she doesn't move so
I rest against her chest
to move with her
finding I can't
as she only touches back
through air
and space

III.

At night I lay alone
grazing the hairs of my arms
touch fingers to bare tips
trying to feel the prints

If the woman at Winco every Thursday
had a zipper to draw along her spine
would she shed her scars
give in to the gift of protruding
ears lips labia and eyelids
instead of the twists of melted flesh
which have enveloped her so long
she has forgotten the face of herself as a child

as if that would erase the burn

Ode to the Very End of Piers

Stuart L. Canton

1.
Walk to the end
from stone, concrete, and sand
to reeking wood and shifting sea
warp and weft of wind and
memory

Run like water from mountains
hours inland to sandstone clefts

Here at the edge
before foaming fathoms
rolling bones towards the shoreline
hear sighs and laments
of the brine

Despite the grimace of the sun
your shadow disappears into the depths

2.
"You can catch fish with marshmallows
as long as they're biting,"
sages teach my brother and me
between sips of coffee
they wait
their lines quiver in the wind

As a child I learned here
I'm drawn back
to the end of the pier
where I sat with my small pole
weighted

It seems answers can be found
where so many cast and wait
where my brother and I sipped cocoa
and shivered in the harsh wind

Waiting for what would come on the other end
the line sunk out of sight

3.
At the beginning
families make photographs
with sunscreen-coated hands
Arm in arm couples laugh
with tones warm as skin

Pizza and beer-battered food
hang greasy in the salted air
Surfboards hurry past
sand grit wet footsteps
running to the billowing surf

As a boy I once found this surf writhing with sand crabs
at the base of the tide
a handful of sand crawled away
small brown waves curling and rolling
the muck filled with life

4.
Walk farther
over water
into silence
Silence felt through
the cry of gulls
hush of waves
moan of wood
thud thud and shink shink of joggers

This is not the tourists' pier
Two teenagers huddle
An old man walks alone
past sinks
bent, mottled with rust
troughs for hot gore to be spilt and returned to the sea
a place to fill buckets with salt water

buckets set next to benches
where people fishing hold their catch

5.
Today, no one is fishing
there is too much sun
Gulls shift their feet back and forth
on the hot, dry boards

The smell of rotted wood
fills the air
drifts back to the beach

A musk of decay
salt and mouldering
scales of fish
smeared across broken barnacles
matted with guano and seal hair

Fresh winds blow sea spray
over the rot

6.
I remember:
I watch a bearded man throw a shining fish onto the pier
too small for him
too big for the gulls

They fight
feet, wings, beaks
slapping and stabbing
the boards with thuds and clicks
The fish sparkles, writhes, flops
One swallows it whole
the others peck the bulge in its neck

7.
The breeze picks up
the pier sways
The land is now the thing at the end of the pier
my kinship with land
pulled out over water

8.
Near the end
often there is one like myself
he puts his sandals back on
and nods as he passes

I step around the bench and onto the ledge
waves tug and push
the water pulls even the sky beneath it

9.
I look down to see my
reflection strangled in kelp
cinched around the poles
There are no easy answers here
there is a rhythm

The flow of the tides
the moaning boards
the reek of death
all moving back and forth
from land to sea to land again
and so I too return to land
and back to the end of the pier
finding my place in the rhythm

Robin

E. Dominguez

I remember the funeral better than the wedding. If it weren't for common sense, I couldn't tell you which came first. Maybe it's from years of miscategorizing memories like a pile of undated photographs. Maybe it's just the narrow window of what I paid attention to, or really *could* pay attention to. It's possible that weddings test my mind in a certain way, as her wedding's just as murky as my own wedding.

The one I recall best is probably Aunt Eli's wedding, her wearing the blue kimono, origami swans on tables, and little kids playing with bubbles—me breaking a lawn chair and Mom threatening to take me home if I didn't stop roughhousing and embarrassing her. Maybe Mom's right, that I cling too closely to the negative events of my life, not enough to the positive. I swear I don't try to.

There's a photo of me at the funeral, wearing a yellow dress, standing by some gravestones, wondering if I should look happy or sad. Was it Aunt Katie who took that photo? My cousin Emily was wandering in the background, so that would make sense. Or maybe that was my sister Mari? Why was it some random gravestones instead of Robin's? In that case, Katie took it. She's spontaneous like that.

The photo at Robin's wedding was much less spontaneous. I was instructed to stand beside my fellow flower girls, Robin crouching down behind us, beaming. She was glad we girls were there on her big day, though little me was disgruntled with the world's most frumpy red thing they called a dress. I hated dresses, will probably never stop hating dresses, and on top of that, the material was itchy. Maybe I missed a lot of the wedding because of that. Uncle was impossibly happy, and Robin's dress complemented her long golden hair, but these thoughts are so vague, I could be thinking of pictures instead of the wedding.

Did I ever mention to them how glad I was they were married, or was I lost in my everyday world? Did I involve myself in the moment when I had the chance? I wonder about this a lot. For many more days than just this.

I knew not to fuss about my dress at the funeral. At least it wasn't chafing. I picked at the skirt in the car, only because it was a dress and for no other particular reason. It was in the car that my mom made her firm views on suicide clear, though I doubt she knew I was listening. (To be fair to her, I didn't know I was listening either.) The topic startled me in a way I didn't understand then. Why was she talking about suicide and Robin

at the same time? Robin's doctor prescribed her a bad dose of medicine. What did that have to do with suicide? Yet Mom went on, about the selfishness, the hurt to everyone around us, the total waste of such potential in life. "And so *young*," she said.

The dots were lined up for me in plain view. Maybe I didn't connect them because I didn't want to. I was only able to deal with her passing at all by keeping thoughts at a surface level. I was accustomed to adults wandering in and out of my life, even braced myself for the eventual "They're moving away" or "We're not friends with them anymore" or "It's complicated." It was only when I considered that she was no longer breathing, that she could be anywhere from Grandpa's Heaven to nowhere at all, that I found it hard to breathe myself. Robin, who'd taught me how to draw stars, played fighter games with me on her computer, danced to "Walk Like an Egyptian," and sang "Roxanne" with me in the back of Grandma's Volkswagen. It was okay for her to be out of my life—she just couldn't be *gone.*

The night of her death, Uncle had come to our house for comfort. He'd sat at the kitchen table, head in his hands, Mom doing her best by sitting beside him. But my little sister, Mari, didn't seem so intent on comforting the man. She kept drawing pictures of Robin and her doing things together, painfully fun and sweet things, and showing Uncle those pictures. I tried to signal her with a glare, but it wasn't until the third picture and my Uncle's third wail that I started yelling at her. I don't know what I said—I doubt I had the vocabulary to convey my fury—but I was louder than I thought myself capable. I made such a ruckus, Dad had to drag me out of the kitchen, into the hall, and give me his Very Stern Dad Voice.

"She's being mean," I told him. "She's making everyone cry again! You shouldn't let her do that!"

"Ellie . . . " he groaned, and I could tell then I was missing something. Again. "This is what people do when somebody dies. They talk about the person and the nice things they remember."

"But they're crying!"

"I know," he said, "but they want to. It helps them feel better."

"Well, it doesn't make *me* feel better!"

Dad grimaced. With his voice calm and level, he told me to go to my room and grieve my own way. I went off, thinking he was disappointed in my inability to understand. I never thought that he just might not know what else to do.

I really didn't understand grieving until I visited Aunt Eli not long before the funeral. My aunt lived in Sacramento then, and while I visited, we went on the first of what would become many aimless walks, talking to each other about life. The subject of Robin came up, and I discovered that Robin was actually Eli's best friend long before Robin and Uncle fell in love. She explained a lot of things I'd never understood before then, like that bipolar had meant Robin was very happy or very sad while growing up. And she told me all sorts of stories and adventures they went on together, with Robin saving the day by seemingly random and inconsequential actions.

My favorite was of Robin going well out of her way to buy a "useless" emergency kit when the two went on

a road trip. It was silly, at least to Eli, that they'd even think of preparing for being stranded when they didn't even plan to stray far from civilization and well-used streets. Yet on the day Robin bought the kit, they took a wrong turn, and their car died in the middle of nowhere, in the snow. And oh, yeah, cell phones weren't a thing. I could picture it clearly in my mind, Robin tugging that gold hair of hers from her face as she brandished the kit from under their seat and declared, "Good thing I brought this along!"

Instead of feeling loss, I felt that I was finding out more about my aunt. And despite the subject, Eli seemed happy to divulge, so I didn't stop her.

"Everything she did," Eli said, "everything that happened around her, I think it all happened for a good reason. Even when she was doing something weird, it turned out for the better in the end. So . . . " She paused a while then. "So I wonder now if there's a reason why this happened."

Encouraged by the stories, I said, "Maybe there is. From all the cool stuff she did . . . Aunt Robin was like a goddess!"

And that made Eli laugh and cry more than I'd like to admit.

I thought about those stories a lot at the funeral and about what Eli said. And since I didn't connect my mother's dots, I kept wondering what good could come from such a horrible accident. I saw even the furthest reaches of my extended family—even those who barely knew Robin—in tears within the pews. And Uncle, he was more broken than I even knew. Soon, he wouldn't be the first person I thought of at the name Uncle, let alone someone I thought of fondly. Distance would eventually change him to "Uncle John," a guy I barely know or see.

Still, all through the funeral, I tried to consider that her profound influence over the world had failed this instance, that for once something had gone wrong and just wrong . . . and I couldn't. I decided that if my grandpa's stories of God's plan had any truth to them, then all of this would have a good effect on us and the world like it always did. It was just that, this time around, the good came at too high a price.

As naive as this solace was, I had no inkling then of how this good could possibly pan out. Or that it would have a direct effect on—of all people—me.

***

I've been told I look cute in my wedding photos. I'm sure I look happy in them too. But I was actually happiest that day walking down the sidewalk. I walked a mile wearing a long, leather coat over my dress, despite the obligatory heat Mexico provided that muggy morning. I was sweating, and I didn't care because I knew I looked awesome in that coat, and it made the dress almost bearable. This dress was handmade just for me by a close friend of my mother-in-law-to-be, Francisca, and she went well out of her way in the instructions to make sure the dress was just the right size, just the right shade of white, had just the right number of flowers embroidered on the skirt. It was so *dainty*, not half as elegant as Robin's, or as bold as Eli's. And, well, it was a *dress*. I couldn't tell anyone I hated it, not even Felipe, the man I was marrying, and I couldn't express my disappointment when they took my coat off for pictures. My hair was as short as a boy's, so I couldn't afford any more

leverage to be myself, especially that day. Every fit he'd thrown when I'd gone to maintain this hair had demonstrated that, and only my nineteen years of age and American heritage excused this rebellion with the locals.

It was a cheap, group wedding that married over a dozen couples at once, one advertised for in flyers, like some kind of fire sale. No one I loved was there to see or support me. All that mattered was that it was functional, that it got this guy into the US, this guy that, frankly, I'd known much better when I was fourteen. Back then, my wacky, homeschool family decided to move to Mexico for a year, becoming neighbors with my great-uncle Pierre, known in the small town of San Juan del Estado (roughly 2,000 people) as the only white man for miles. At the time, Felipe had already proven a great deal of loyalty while working for Pierre at an Internet café, and was practically his right-hand man. Felipe and his family bonded well with mine long before we started dating, and once we had, my family seemed excited for me in a way they'd never been before. *Oooh, a boy likes Ellie. Can you believe it? Look at that!*

Then, of course, we returned to the US and Felipe was desperate to follow us, yet my parents couldn't find a way. Sponsorship? No, we'd have to be related. Citizenship? No, that cost more money than we all had combined. Work? Ha, ha, cute idea. My mother's voice was depressing enough when she had to tell the eighteen-year-old boy that his only way in was across the border. And to my horror, she agreed to help any way she could if he ultimately decided to do it. I begged him to wait for me to get out of high school, feeling like I was the only one who knew how dangerous it was, but Felipe said he just couldn't wait that long. So in the midst of my sophomore year, my mother drove down to San Diego to pick him up off the side of the road, finding him alone, shirtless, and in tears. He told me of that journey so many times, of how his group had been robbed at gunpoint (even taking his shirt) and how skinheads had shot at them, and he'd had to leave a wounded man behind—and that was just the first half of his trek.

He was never the same after that. But he was never the same because of me. How do you turn away from someone who's been traumatized because of you? But, of course, he hadn't been able to live up to his potential being undocumented, which my parents couldn't allow to continue. To not have him as a son was a tragedy, yet they could compromise with him as their son-in-law. So when I saw how expensive a school like UCLA would be and felt that my dream to be a novelist wouldn't exactly cover the costs, it made sense to have my dad drive us down to Tijuana and let me fly the rest of the way to San Juan, my new home for however long it would take to tie the knot.

This was the day that would fix everything. We'd be able to go back home where he'd have better opportunities for his future. Where he wouldn't get away with the broken promises that started once we lived together. Where he would stop cursing at me for my lack of Spanish. Where he couldn't brush off my crush on the cashier with, "You're not really gay, Elena, you just want to be gay." And maybe he'd stop using that stupid pet name too. After this, life would be better. He would be better. Everything would be.

It had to be.

I ducked into the bathroom three or four times as we waited for everyone to assemble, checking to make sure I wasn't about to menstruate as the abdominal pain suggested. Part of me was hoping something like that would go wrong, wrong enough that it would stop. The sweltering, paperless bathroom stall was more comfort-

ing than what waited outside. The wedding itself didn't matter. I kept telling myself over and over, "It doesn't matter. It's going to be okay. I can do this. I can do this, I can do this."

Everything he'd done and everything I wanted weren't matching up. I wanted to forge my own path through school, work, anything, yet this was contradictory to the actions leading me to this stall. I didn't feel I had the strength to stand on my own, and even then I didn't want to be alone the rest of my life. Though the dots were laid out in plain sight, I refused to connect them. I didn't have the strength to admit this was wrong. I couldn't bear to admit I didn't love him anymore.

Mom was proud of me, of this. The kid too dumb to understand basic human interaction, like how to behave at a wedding, the one with "suspiciously" selective hearing and no sense of attention control, the one who couldn't remember what day it was or even tell left from right—Mom was proud of *me.* And despite that, I wanted to run out to a taxi and to the airport and drop pesos in a phone booth and leave a message saying, I couldn't, I tried, but I couldn't, I'm sorry, I'm *sorry,* I just need to come back and forget that this happened. But the image of me standing in the San Francisco airport, alone because they were too bothered with disappointment to come get me—no, leaving came at too high a price.

That's what I take with me out of the stall. That's what keeps me holding his hand as I say, "*Siii,*" half a beat off from the rest of the girls because I don't know what the pastor's even saying.

***

The thin metal tracks of the light rail start to whistle before I can even see the train. I'm standing on the yellow plastic of the platform that makes me think of Legos, telling myself everything's going to be okay, I'm okay. I can still find someone in Midtown to interview, finish the article due tonight, still salvage this internship, still salvage this life I gave up my mother for. "I can do this, I can do this. It's going to be okay." But inside my head, my voice is different. My mom was right to call me a monster and cast me out, just like I thought she would. I was right to think I couldn't stand on my own, make my own way. My future holds nothing but welfare and cats, and just the act of standing here, trying, is selfish. I can't even utilize a full week to get *one* interview. I'm a horrible person and even more horrible at trying to be one.

The pressure builds into the top of my head until it caves in, and I find myself outside of the world around me, just like when I was a kid. This place is dark, twisted, and feels endless—like I was never anywhere else before and will never be anywhere else again. That extra step forward onto the light rail track is the only way out. And it might even be the best way. To this day, there's debate on whether Robin's overdose was intentional or not, and with my inabilities, maybe this way would leave the same debate open. If I can't live a decent life for my family . . .

The train's on its way. I have the exact amount of time I need to make either decision. In the dark, my future's set in stone, much like my past. I'm a disappointment. A failed business investment. A broken piece of shit. My own goals have gotten me nowhere but into a crap internship with a news blog I don't even like, an area of writing I don't even like. And with how well I'm doing, my hopes of getting hired are slim to none. I've wasted their time, the staff's time, the time my aunt's given me in their spare room, the time my grandmother's

given me on her couch, just as I wasted every damn second of time I spent growing up writing fantasy stories and dating a boy that would grow up a different man. The only saving grace I have is that I can still shove on a dress and look happy for the camera, if I'm not too stubborn to do so. But no, now even that's not enough. If I pretend this was a phase and go crawling back to Mexico, it'll only be an example for others to follow. How many people, even mild acquaintances, told me I appeared to be living happily ever after? How many would hurt themselves striving for the lie I'd created, say they went through "rough patches" like me? I have enough people looking up to me, with my five siblings alone, people rooting for me and believing in me enough to offer a couch—I can't lie to them anymore. Even Felipe still deserves someone who actually loves him, which I've failed to do. That was the *only* chance life gave me, and I fucked it up.

Either my family suffers me living, or they suffer me dying. Both acts feel selfish and wrong now, and I can't tell which is the higher price.

I think about all the things given to me, all the things spent on my worthless life: cereal bowls full of dimes, the mountain of cash on my computer desk—all the things my parents, siblings, friends could have done without me there to drain their resources. Without me there to burden them with my broken brain and misplaced emotions, emotions I don't even understand, Mari could have gone to choir again, and Jette could have taken that theater class. I don't even know if I'm a gay woman or a straight woman or a bisexual man or even human anymore. I don't get to tell people I think I find them attractive because I can't take it back if it turns out I'm wrong. I can't take it back, but I can keep it from continuing. I can stop pretending that I'll ever manage on my own, that I can ever contribute to the world. I just need the right step at the right time.

I think about the pews full of heartbroken people, the virtual loss of my uncle. Robin wasn't much older than I am, was she? They're going to say I was so young. Even if I'm right, and this is still what's best for them in the long run, it's still going to sting. Goddammit, my youngest brother's three years old. I'm not Aunt Robin. I'm no goddess. But what if my death *does* hurt them, like it hurt Uncle John, Aunt Eli, everyone? What the hell could I do then? Can I even do *this* without screwing it up, without surviving and costing *more* in medical bills? Why can't someone just fix what's wrong with me? Why do I have to stand here, alone?

My feet lock to the Lego platform as the light rail train rolls by. It's not that I don't want to step. It's that I'm at a stalemate. I mechanically march up the train steps and into a seat, reeking of sweat, as my mind surfaces from the dark. Suddenly, I'm thinking like a self-preserving human again, reeling in amazement at what I was considering, then realize this is going to happen again and again, until I make the choice I can't take back. It doesn't matter if I think I'm right if I'm wrong, if I try to solve the problem and only make things worse. I've learned that much from my mistakes.

I can't carry on like this. I don't trust myself to. I need help, and I need it now.

I cry a lot on the train. I consider waiting another day for getting help, making that last jab at finding an interview instead, but this isn't something I can shrug off and forget to do. That'll just give strength to the dark, another chance to take me out. I get off in Midtown, walk to an isolated corner and whip out my phone, searching through my contacts. I need to get help. Each name I read is just a voice screaming in outrage. One is accusing me of looking for attention. Then it's being selfish. Then being stupid. *God, Ellie,* I picture them saying, *do you need to do this now?* I search through a third time, reconsidering, but this is too big a burden to

put on someone who'd *want* to help me.

I want Robin's number in my phone. I want to call her and spill out unintelligible blathering. I want her to blaze a trail to come and get me where I stand, and to tell me I'm going to be okay. Don't move a muscle, you're not in trouble, it's all right. *I understand,* she'd say. *I understand.*

But I don't have Robin. I just have some old photographs. Her memory was what stabilized me, what held me fast to the Lego floor, but it's not enough and never could be, not when she could be here.

As I hold the phone and think of what's happened, of the solace I found at her funeral, I'm flooded with the thought I don't want: maybe, maybe this is it. Would I have stayed put if I hadn't thought of her death, of how it hurt others, of the life she could have lived? Would I want to call her now if she hadn't died? If this is it, if this is just another episode of Goddess Robin to the Rescue, my life and sanity couldn't possibly be worth Robin's life. The price is too fucking high, and I'm insulted at myself.

But if it is, and I know there's a *chance* that it is, then I can't let it go to waste. I have to salvage something from this mess of a life—any way I can. Because if this *is* why my aunt took her life, then she *is* worth all that I can give. Even if it doesn't amount to enough, it can still amount to something. Amounting to nothing and throwing my life away now would be the true insult to her memory.

I still have no one to call. So I call 911.

Vacancy

Kourtney Holloman

I am waiting to lose you.
Familiar smile
left decaying,
eyes yellow, hollow.
Skin pulled tight, paper thin,
flesh hangs barely to bone—
to dance atop your feet again
I'd surely break them.

It's hard to look at you, to see
not the what, but the who
that's been lost—
former conqueror of midnight,
monsters, and bedtime shadows.
Body now reeks of tequila
and death—
it's telling you something.
You don't listen.

When the pain begins to bleed back in
you reach for your bottle,
not for the high—there is no high left for you,
just numbness.

I sit through the blur of home movies,
watch your breath help carry my wish
of another day with you in the park
to three pink candles.

But you stumble by,
hair and clothes tattered,
unable to recognize I am in the room.

I sit—
waiting to lose
the absence of you.

Double Radical

Elaine Lenore

For years she had lain naked with him
Now she wears a high-collared flannel gown
hiding scars like vertical zippers
on a concave chest
which she had bound in her past
choosing to abandon her natural jiggle
in favor of androgyny, the flapper aesthetic

At bacchanalian parties
she'd roll down her stockings
kick off her shoes
Charleston
a swing and a blur of purple fringe

Now she stands before him
Her gown drops to the floor
With a familiar appraising look
his eyes let her know without doubt
it's true
he always was
more of a leg man

Thoughts from the Commode

Tiffany Bush

Two squares. Left to her own devices, that's the exact amount of toilet paper my grandmother chooses. It's not an accident, either. She deliberately counts them—one, two—and then gently separates the delicate paper from the roll. It doesn't matter how messy she is. Anything more than two is a waste.

She's 95 years old, walks with a walker, and has an oxygen tank. She wears hearing aids and laughs when she doesn't hear what you say. She goes to bed at 8 p.m., even if she's slept all day. And she only uses two squares of toilet paper.

One of the first known instances of the use of toilet paper was by a Chinese emperor in 1391. Toilet paper was a luxury item. It was a two-foot by three-foot sheet of cloth. The Bureau of Imperial Supplies began producing the sheets, up to 720,000 a year. These were distributed mostly to the emperor, as many citizens could not afford them.

It's a good bet the emperor didn't wipe his own bum, since such a task was beneath him, so the large size probably came in handy for his assistants.

My grandmother was born in England in 1919. At the end of World War II, when she came to the United States with my grandfather, she brought along some of her heritage. One word I can remember her using frequently was "loo." She even had a small plaque on the bathroom door with the word on it. She never had to use the bathroom or the restroom or the toilet. She would simply say, "I have to pay a penny to the loo." I never questioned it.

The first flushing toilet was introduced in 1596. Its creator, Sir John Harrington, was a British nobleman and the godson of Queen Elizabeth I, and he often suggested flushing at least twice a day—a bit low for today's standards. This incredible toilet required a simple pull of a handle to empty water from a cabinet, and this water would wash the business away. This is why when it was first invented it was called the water closet.

Although no one knows for sure, there is some speculation that the nickname "the john" is in reference to Sir John Harrington himself.

Rationing took its toll on the World War II populace. Even with rationing gone, many World War II veterans and survivors still have the mentality that things need to be saved and reused, or minimalized, something younger generations in this throw-away world don't seem to understand. My grandmother is no exception to this. She washes out sandwich bags to reuse them. She hides extra money in the hems of her clothes. And she only uses two squares of toilet paper in the loo.

The average person spends a total of three years of his life on the toilet. This is a lot of time in

one place, and humans have discovered innovative ways to help pass the time. One way commonly depicted in comics and movies is to bring a newspaper along to catch up on business while doing your business. Another way to occupy time on the porcelain throne is to buy themed toilet paper. It now comes in a variety of colors and prints, including Sudoku. This makes it possible to keep your brain sharp in an otherwise dull situation. Fill out your puzzle, and then wipe yourself clean with it.

The newest innovation to help pass the time on the john is the cell phone. Boredom no longer exists. Play games, text friends, even call them to say hello. In extreme circumstances, the cell phone can even tell you if your most recent feces sample is healthy or not.

When my grandmother first started to lose her independence, she would fight with my mother, her caretaker, about everything—doctor appointments, using the walker, the way food was prepared. The proper amount of toilet paper to use was no exception to this, and she fought hard for her two squares. If my mother handed her more, she'd tear off her portion and hand the excess back, saying, "Here, you can waste it."

Toilet paper is no longer just a cleaner for your behind. It has evolved to be more versatile in its usage. It's used for blowing noses; though not as soft as facial tissue, it holds up just as well under pressure. It's used to clean up messes; after all, that's why it was invented, right? In a pinch, it can be used for packing material. It can even be festive. On Halloween, it can be used to turn a person into a mummy, or you can throw it all over the yard of the house where they skimped on the candy.

In 2005, a new use for toilet paper was discovered: clothing. A contest was announced, and using nothing but toilet paper, glue, and tape, contestants were challenged to create the best wedding dress. The contest was such a hit, it became an annual event.

My grandmother would see all of this folly as a waste of good toilet paper.

In the US, we see toilet paper as a necessity, but the truth is that it's not. Four billion people, about seventy percent of Earth's population, still do not use toilet paper. The reasons vary. For some, it is a matter of religious belief. For others, it is a lack of trees to produce the product. A lot of the world's population finds this first-world commodity too expensive and would rather not spend so much money on fancy paper to wipe their behinds. Perhaps people in the US understand the pricing issue better than we think. After all, this is the land of opportunity, and seven percent of hotel guests take the opportunity to acquire rolls of toilet paper from their rooms.

Over the years, my grandmother taught me many things. She taught me about love and kindness, responsibility, and owning up to one's mistakes. She taught me honesty, how to appreciate nature, and conservation. And she taught me that I will never use just two squares of toilet paper.

For anything.

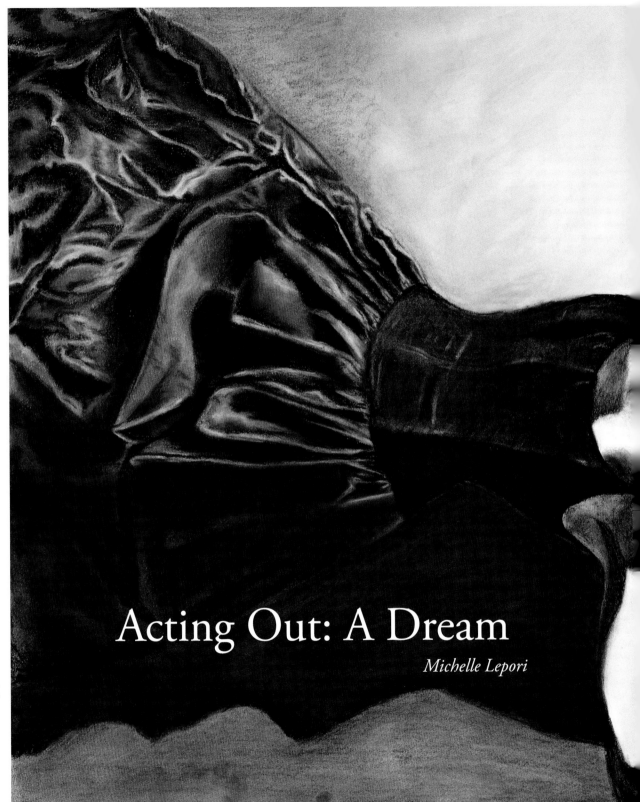

Acting Out: A Dream

Michelle Lepori

Upon closer inspection, her lips, dark

from shadow play cast by curtains

of red curls and window pane glasses,

were alligator skin green.

Were they larger, I would kill her

and fashion a coin purse—but not to hold

change, her lips too loose

to keep value. She was a theatre

of truth. Her demands to *act now!*

I heard in a hush, as if we were being

watched. I stared at this dream woman,

at her captured youth, framed many times.

Her celebrity hung on the wall like rope from trees.

October Surprise

Diane McCarthy

October, 1980. Fifty-two hostages. The success or failure to free them would decide the next US presidential election. Some believe the Reagan/Bush campaign made a secret deal with their captors to delay their release. Some even claim the deal was closed at a clandestine meeting in Paris attended by George H. W. Bush. To this day, despite serious investigation, this claim cannot be ruled out.

George thought he must have misunderstood. Thank-you notes? Had he really heard, I want you to write thank-you notes? Perhaps it was that he hadn't actually *heard* it. This way of communicating was something he was going to have to get used to. He'd just finish forming a question in his mind, and then the answer would just *be* there. But he thought if he had the answer all along, why did he have to ask the question in the first place? And that was just one of the puzzling things about this place.

The room was cold and dank, and there were no windows. George guessed it was underground, which would explain why the air was so stale. The walls were mushroom-colored. There was no one else in the room, but he heard voices outside somewhere speaking a language he could not understand. He had heard the language before but couldn't place it.

All he could really remember was the machine in the hospital with the oscillating green line and thinking that the doctors in their masks, gowns, and caps had been covered even more completely than a woman in a chador. He remembered feeling frightened that he could see only their eyes and not their faces. They had been shouting to each other, but then their shouting had become more and more distant until he hadn't been able to hear them at all.

He got up from the bed and tried moving around to get warmer, but the cold came right up from the floor through his bare feet. He wondered why he didn't have any shoes. You don't need shoes, he thought. Then he frowned. How did he know this? It was like knowing he was supposed to write thank-you notes. He walked over to the small, wooden table and chair in the middle of the room. The chair was flimsy and had no cushion. There was a clear, non-retractable Bic pen and some blank 3″ x 5″ cards on the table. Cheap stationery. He picked up the cards and counted them. Fifty-two.

George walked back to the bed and lay down. Someone would have to be by soon to bring him some food, he decided, and he would just wait and ask them some questions. Except, thinking about it, it must have been hours since he'd eaten because he didn't recall having a meal. And yet, he wasn't hungry. Or thirsty. It's just that it was so cold. He suddenly felt very drowsy, but he struggled to stay awake because he heard the voices getting closer. At last he could talk to someone, he thought.

. . .

It was very peculiar, this sleeping with your eyes open. It was more like watching a movie and not restful at all. In this strange movie, a mass of foreign-looking men, scary in their intensity, were storming what looked like a ransacked building. They were pouring in over a wall and through the windows and pounding and stomping so loudly that the building shook as if there were an earthquake. A group of them raced down a corridor, a door opened to a room, and it grew quiet. Inside, a man with a hood over his head, and his hands tied behind his back, sat on a stool surrounded by men with faces purple with anger. George was glad he wasn't there, but then he thought he must be for he realized it … *smelled.* There was a strong unpleasant stench of body odor.

George suddenly couldn't see a thing and could barely breathe through the heavy cloth covering his face. His shoulders ached from the way his hands were tied behind his back, the knotted rope digging painfully into his wrists, and his hands felt sharp, stinging pricks from lack of circulation. He was very thirsty, and yet he felt a powerful need to urinate, but he was too terrified to ask for anything. He heard voices arguing in that language he'd heard before, and although he couldn't understand what they were saying, he was certain the men wanted to harm him. They seemed to be quarrelling about what to do with him when an ear-splitting curse and a powerful blow to his jaw exploded simultaneously. Then two, maybe three of them, set upon him—screaming taunts, and kicking him in his ribs, his back, his kidneys—with no finesse, but the pain, exquisite. Someone threw a bucket of cold water over him and left him shaking, each shiver like a thousand needles of fire and ice.

. . .

George woke with a scream. Or rather, his mouth was open as if he'd been screaming, but there was no sound. The memory of his dream was clear in his mind, but he couldn't tell if his jaw actually hurt, or if he was only feeling the memory of it hurting. He remembered the ice-cold water and was surprised to find he wasn't wet. And odd too, he was no longer thirsty nor did he have to urinate. Then the voices he had heard before started chanting, but infuriatingly, they'd get softer each time he actually tried to make out the words. He was certain he had heard that language before. The drone of the voices was mesmerizing, and he started feeling tired again but got up from the bed. He did not want to have another dream.

The table and chair yawned at him, and he sat down. Fifty-two cards. Okay, he could make a deck of cards and play solitaire. At least that would put a dent in the boredom. But as he put the pen to a card to draw the face of a king, what felt like an electric shock ran up his arm. He dropped the pen, and it skittered and bounced off the table. George inspected the table where the pen had landed and saw deep burn marks on the surface. He found himself knowing: not playing cards, thank-you notes. The pen was on the floor, and he bent down to retrieve it gingerly. He picked up one of the cards. He wrote, *Dear,* and paused to search his memory. He remembered there had been doctors trying to help him, but he no longer had memory of any of them, just the blur of their green gowns. Still. Maybe he was supposed to thank them for having been concerned. But surely there hadn't been fifty-two of them.

George was getting tired again. He decided he would lie down on the bed and not actually sleep. But the moment he lay down he found himself yawning. The voices started chanting louder, and their rhythmic sound dragged him into a stupor. He saw a man, dressed in rags, lying face down in a dark prison cell. He couldn't tell who the man was in the dim light.

. . .

George again felt his wrists tied behind him, but this time he was not blindfolded. As his eyes adjusted to near total darkness, he saw he was lying on a Styrofoam mat on a cement floor. He was alone, but foul-smelling puddles in the corners of the cell suggested previous occupants. Just outside the steel door he could hear a tinny radio playing classical music. An abrupt hush in the music let him hear the sound of a whip hitting skin and a man's terrible cry. After another hideous scream, the music was turned up so loud it was distorted. George knew the man must still be screaming, and not being able to hear it was disconcerting. Somewhere down a hall he heard a metal door swing open and shut. He could not think which was worse—the fear that someone would soon come for him or the fear that he was completely forgotten and no one would ever come for him. He considered this for a very long time but could not decide, which made the fear escalate, and sleep elude him.

. . .

But he must have fallen asleep. Otherwise he couldn't now be waking. He thought maybe he had heard someone about to come in and looked for the steel door but saw there wasn't any door, only four identical walls. He was back in the room with the table and chair, and there was no music anymore and no smell. Funny he hadn't noticed before that the room didn't have a door. How the heck had he gotten in? Then George had the answer in his mind, but the answer was so terrible he pretended he didn't know it, and then suddenly, he didn't even remember what he had been thinking. He went over to the table and sat down. Fifty-two cards, fifty-two thank-you notes. And since a note had to be *to* someone, that meant fifty-two people. But he couldn't remember even one person he could write.

As his mind drifted, he forgot to stop himself from wondering about who the fifty-two people might be, and instantly, he had a picture in his mind of a hotel room. He could tell from the electrical outlets and the ornate furniture that the room was not in America. He guessed somewhere in Europe, though he wasn't certain since the shades were drawn. The room was well-lit, but it was filled with shadows. The shadows solidified into forms, and the forms coalesced into people.

. . .

The Louis XIV-style chair was damned uncomfortable, and it was all George could do to keep from fidgeting. The other people in the room seemed both relieved and anxious, like they were close to wrapping up a big business deal that could still go wrong. At first he couldn't quite place them. Except for one or two, they weren't European. Mostly they were something else, Middle Eastern maybe, and a couple could only be Americans. Only one of them seemed like someone he'd ever want to have a drink with, a tall, stooped, white-haired guy who was insisting, "No, not in October, not until January!"

The foreign-looking men exchanged wary glances then spoke rapidly among themselves in the language he'd heard before. Finally they said, "Okay. Three more months, all fifty-two."

That was when something flew out of George and settled into the form of a crow. The crow rested on his shoulder and grew larger and larger until he was eclipsed, just a tiny thing, and the crow flew off with a great flapping of wings.

. . .

The sound of flapping wings startled him, but when he woke he was alone again in the mushroom-

colored room. He knew all at once who the fifty-two people were and that it was going to be hard to write them thank-you notes. He sat at the wooden table and squirmed as he rifled through the stack of blank cards. Then he had a wild thought: could an apology get him out of here? The answer was immediate and harsh.

Gritting his teeth, he picked up his pen and wrote: *Dear*—George couldn't think of any of their names—*Friend. I wish to express my appreciation to you and your colleagues. Thank you*—he considered how best to put this delicately—*for the opportunity you gave me to serve my country. As the strongest, freest nation in the world we owe it to the free nations of the world to lead, to stay strong, to care. Sincerely.* Then he signed his name.

George didn't see why he couldn't write the same thing on the other cards, so he copied the same message over and over. He noticed that the black ink in the pen was running low, and he wondered if he'd be able to get through all the cards before it ran out. After he finished all but one, he shook the pen vigorously, but when he stopped shaking it he saw with astonishment that the pen was totally replenished with ink. Then, he saw that the card he'd just written was now blank, and all of the other cards were blank too.

It was taxing to write the notes all over again, but George was careful this time to handle each card gingerly and to not shake the pen. He'd started writing each a little differently to personalize them. On one he added, *Take comfort in knowing you served your country with courage, honor, and pride,* and on another, he decided to add some helpful advice that he wished he'd been more careful to follow: *Tell the truth. Don't blame people. Be strong. Do your best. Try hard. Forgive. Stay the course.* He was nearly done, each card placed carefully after the next in neat rows. He took a moment to rub his eyes, but when he opened them he saw rows and rows of blank cards and the pen refilled with ink. The chanting started again, and this time the cadence was spritely, as if to mock him.

This was too much, thought George. This shall not stand. He picked up the pen defiantly and wrote on the top card: *To whom it may concern: I can categorically assure you that I was never a participant in a scheme to keep any American held hostage. Please accept my word that I know nothing about anyone else's involvement in such an insidious plot. I wish you all the best, and I hope this has laid to rest some of your understandable concerns.*

He waited, but for a moment there was nothing. Then, one after another, the words he'd written slid off the card, and the card was blank and empty as before. The words dissolved into a splash of black ink that started to dance like spilled mercury, expand, and coalesce until its blackness filled the room. Something surrounded him, black and indistinguishable from the rest of the blackness, and he could feel its crushing pressure on his chest. At last the Being breathed one word, and as George turned the word over and over in his mind in awe, infinitesimally tiny pieces of the word spun off in brilliant bursts of light that sparkled and fell in the darkness. Suddenly, he too was falling at tremendous, gathering speed, past darkness, past worlds, until just as he thought he must shatter into an untold number of particles and dust, he felt himself caught by a great invisible hand that set him down with great care.

He opened his eyes to find that he had landed in the bed in the mushroom-colored room. From somewhere in his mind he heard, thank-you notes. I want you to write thank-you notes. George got up slowly, shuffled over to the table, and sat down.

Rangda

Anique Bailey

It feels like meditation, an out-of-body experience. Astral projection to nowhere in particular. Moonwalking. Her sister drives, and in the back is everything she cares to keep: a suitcase, a lamp shaped like a turtle, two pairs of shoes, a sachet of pills, and a Spider-Man coffee mug her nephew gave her before he could really pick out anything that wasn't for him. The car is one of those new quiet models, soundproofed against itself and the world. She twists the gold band on her finger, false and feigning, and watches people on mute: mowing their lawns, trimming their hedges, walking their frantic dogs. Twist. Everything is slow. Everything but her sister, amped and rattling away at the wheel, outlining the next six months like the last six never happened. A slow, inevitable kind of degeneration.

"We can get the rest of your stuff, the heavy stuff, when you feel better. There's no hurry to get back to work. Your boss has been plenty understanding through all this and is extending your leave. So whenever you feel like it, Mike or I can drive you until you can start driving again."

Sheila has fallen back into concerned big sister like a welcome trap. Next to Shela she feels dark and small like she's been quarantined. She inspects her frayed cuticles, listening with mild obedience, her mind in a mute white room.

*

Mike isn't home, but Conner, now old enough to not evaluate the world by how it relates to Peter Parker, is. He acts like he's never seen her in his life, and she realizes, as Sheila tries to jog his memory, that he most likely hasn't. Three months old doesn't count, and she sent all his birthday presents FedEx. She wonders if Sheila would have shown the same disinterest had their places been reversed.

Sheila finally gives up in classic TV Land style, hands in the air and a shake of her head.

"Okay, fine, whatever. Conner, you better not leave that table until you finish your homework. I'm going to go settle Lena into the guest room, then I'll be back to make dinner." He rolls his eyes, too old and too cool to be polite. She doesn't know if he is especially advanced or if all fifth graders are like this. She trails after her sister, thumb smoothing over the lamp's turtle head. She'll probably never know.

*

The room is small and square and every inch a guest bedroom. It tells her pleasant hellos, mumbles polite limitations, hints at comfortable stays of time, *both for you and me*. It says, considerately, *I have other things to do as well, and you have a life you need to get back to, don't you?*

She sticks her lamp on the nightstand and leaves it unplugged.

The way to the hall bathroom is a tunnel of bizarre masks and strange fetishes, foreign faces peering blankly at travelers. She's snagged by bulging eyes and a grin of thick teeth.

If this is anyone's fault, it says, a pleasant growl, *it's his.*

The rest of the alien faces stay mum, but they agree. She agrees.

*

"The mask?" Her sister echoes, eyebrow cocked in that genetic way only she was ever able to master. It takes Sheila a moment to sort through her memory of the hallway decor and find the one her sister is talking about. They're at the dinner table, eating a quick meal before Conner has to go back to doing homework. Mike still isn't home yet. She wonders if maybe her sister isn't in such a different place from her after all. "Oh. Right. One of the ugly ones. Uncle Jaime, you remember Jaime, right? The one with the loud voice and the rosacea on his neck? He went to some Indonesian country one summer and gave me that mask when he came back." She quirks her mouth and shrugs. "He gave me just about everything in that hall. Never told him not to, so the things just kept coming."

She remembers Uncle Jaime. She had never liked him, and he had never tried to change that. She toys with her box linguini and waits for her sister to continue. Sheila doesn't disappoint. "I think it's part of a good and evil ritual. The evil god terrorizes the villagers until the good god comes out and sends it packing. Anyway, that mask is the evil god. I forgot the name. Raida, Rawanda, I don't know, something like that, I'm terrible at names. I guess that applies to names of heathen gods too."

She asks if maybe Sheila could ask Jaime more about it, and Sheila waves her fork around noncommittally and badgers her son into sitting up straight.

*

Mike comes home hours later, nods at her as she sits in one of their strategically placed easy chairs, and goes to rummage for leftovers in the kitchen. Conner and Sheila had gone to bed a long time ago. She had tried and failed, lain under the politely hostile coverlet and traced shadows streaking across the ceiling, traced ridges and surgical stitches across her belly, traced the past into a future that would never happen.

When Mike goes to bed she takes her turn in the kitchen, filling a glass with water from the tap. Half-blind in the dark, she carefully pops the lid on the bottle, rolls a pill out, and places it dead center on her tongue. She drains the glass, leaves it on the counter, and wanders back towards the guest room, changes her mind and goes to the bathroom instead. She hovers by the mask, tries pinpointing where its eyes would be, imagines black holes hiding on the walls.

You're mopey, it tells her, smooth and humming. *Nobody likes a Debbie Downer. He didn't.*

Its entourage hums her out of the hallway and she goes to bed without peeing, hands curled close around her stitched and aching belly.

*

Sheila is bullying Conner around the kitchen in the morning, hounding him at every pause. Mike is still asleep, and she can't remember what it is he does that keeps him out so late and lets him sleep in so long. She's

sitting at the kitchen island, hands wrapped around her Spider-Man mug full of coffee, watching Sheila be a machine of a mom. She wonders where her sister picked that up. Conner's eyes seem to be in perma-roll, and the only sounds he makes are irritated sighs. She thinks if Sheila doesn't lay off soon, she's going to degenerate into one of those mothers who never severs the cord.

The only time Sheila stops her rampage is to inform her that while she has to run some errands she'll be home just after nine-ish, ten-ish, eleven-ish, something like that. Mike will be up in an hour or two. Don't try to talk to him until he has something to eat, has shaved, has resumed his human status.

"Just relax," her sister says, fighting with Conner and a backpack, "Just sit back and don't worry about anything. No extraneous activity, doctor's orders. Literally, Lena. You seem to have a problem with this."

She flexes her fingers around Spider-Man and nods.

Just as Sheila's stepping out the door, she adds, "I remember, about the mask now. It's a witch, I think, a child-eating widow."

And then her sister's gone, and the house is muffled and she is alone. She twists her ring, takes her prescriptions dry this time, and ignores the dull throb in her pelvis.

*

Drumming in her ears, her tremulous tribal heartbeat. She watches the mask out of the corner of her eye, face averted, incognito. It knows she's watching anyway, smiles, calls to her.

You never took the time to appreciate what you had, it sings with its backup chorus. *But neither did he.*

*

When Mike shuffles into the kitchen she's back at the island, hands wrapped around Spider-Man again, only now the coffee in it, untouched, is dead cold. She is in orbit right now. Mike drains the coffee pot and starts it up again, and while that's going, he grabs ice cream from the freezer, Cheetos from behind the cereal, and Pop-Tarts from the cabinet above the fridge.

She dislodges from her space station and watches, in strange fascination, as he eats a quarter of the Mint Madness carton and two foil packages of fudge Pop-Tarts. He refills his coffee cup and tugs Spider-Man out of her fingers. He dumps the old and fills it with new and nestles it easy and soft back into her palms. He leaves and she stares at the cup in her hands, steaming into the slightly colder air.

There are still some Cheetos left, and she wonders if that was on purpose.

*

Sounds of Sheila's homecoming filter in from the living room front entrance. Soft curses and the rustling of plastic grocery bags. The coffee has gone cold again. She hears her sister talking in furtive whispers with her husband in the living room, low tones for nosy guests. She can hear the slow, sly beating of her sluggish heart in her ears. She can hear the soft warning chuckle drifting from the dark hallway. She hears nothing from the nothingness in her pelvis.

Sheila troops into the kitchen and unloads her treasures. Wordless, Mike follows, helping the least amount possible. He refreshes her coffee a second time and drifts back out of the kitchen. Sheila stays in the kitchen even

after everything is put away, puttering around in an alienly maternal fashion.

She is miles away, a stranger looking in, watching a woman in her kitchen and a girl made of clay beside her. She is fathoms deep, taking in water.

*

Mike has left for work, Sheila on another short–I–promise errand and now everything hurts. The black hole at her center is eating up what she is, what she was, and spilling out throbbing pain in return. She is unraveling, and she is doing the unraveling. She twists her ring, pops the top on her bottle.

The coffee is still warm, so she drinks that and three pills.

*

At some point she manages to wander into the hallway bathroom. She stares at her reflection, gaunt and flat in the mirror. Her hair hasn't been brushed in weeks (days months years), and her skin is smeared dark under her eyes, a mark of her plasticky stasis of unbeing; her nails are long and curved or short and saw-toothed. She scowls at her other self, draws her tongue out long, scrapes at the film covering it, and thinks about the mask in the hallway.

*

You know, it whispers through its chunky-toothed smile, *he was just waiting for an excuse to get rid of you.*

It comes off the wall with a moment of resistance, easy and eager in her hands. The strap fits against the curve of her skull, tucked behind her ears. She looks out through bulging eyes and tusked grimace, and agrees, agrees, agrees.

*

She smashes the cup onto the countertop—hot, black coffee dribbling over the edge onto the floor. Shards sliver-slip into her hand. Her ring flashes false in the light and she thinks about what a uterus looks like, what hers looks like, scarred and broken. What her husband's future wife's will look like, what their kids will look like, what their life will look like.

She smashes another cup, Mike's, left out like everything else, and twists, twists-twists her ring right off. She drops it down into the black-hole void of the garbage disposal and flips the switch. It sputters the mangled ring up and out; the disposal in electro-humming semi-sentience, knowing it is on, but it is broken.

She starts laughing, the sound muffled and low through the mask, and by the time her sister comes home, her bottle of pills is empty and she's digging through her stitches to see what her uterus really looks like now that it's useless.

Leftovers

Isabel Geerer

Ants moved into the house the winter after he moved out. A single scout unobtrusively checked the terrain, then returned with an invasion. They crawled out of the tub drain like cockroaches, framed windows and doors, clogged cracks and crevices.

She fought them off with bleach, feeling it was less toxic than bug spray, and searched for what they were after. No one was making a mess but her. She kept the crumbs swept off the floor; washed, dried, and put away dishes after using them, usually eating over the sink before and after work.

The last thing she saw when leaving every morning was the relentless barrage of ants marching single file across the welcome mat, entering the house through a hidden chink in the weather stripping around the front door. In the evening, she wiped away trails of ants streaming in from every entry point in the house, scoured the toilet and tub, wiped the sink and mirror, and combed the rest of the house for whatever was drawing them 'til bed.

Saturday morning, she pulled his mug from the cabinet, the one that kept coffee hot the longest. She used to try to get it before he woke up. She sat at the table wondering what to do. The refrigerator hummed. No one needed anything from her. Contemplating the cruelty of abandoning one's favorite receptacle, she took a sip. Inside, an ant floated like a stray coffee ground.

Looking up from the mug, she saw ants in a single, stitched seam bordering the hall. She followed them to the bedroom closet and opened the door. Ants unraveled flesh from not-so-dry bones. The empty eye sockets of her former self glared. She shut the door.

Hrunting

Anique Bailey

Sammy wake up. This is what you say to yourself, but really to her. Sammy wake up. For nine long, empty hours you plead the floor, and you'll plead nine more, if that's what it takes, if that's what makes this better. You sit stiff and silent by her side, neck bent, eyes wide, dry, waiting, staring, praying, though you don't really know how to pray. You hope you're doing it right. You hope you aren't just pissing off the powers that be and that these past nine hours haven't just been to get back at your awkward Hail Mary or your half-assed Buddhist chants. You hope she wakes up, and you hope she's okay, that everything's okay, because no one's told you a damn thing since you got here, so you've had to run on faith (and maybe you've run as far as you can).

*

Denver throws Carla's purse off an overpass and watches three cars smash it to bits, watches a fourth try to avoid handbag shrapnel, but it's too late, that shit is gone—gone and good riddance. He ignores Carla and Carla's furious squawk-squeals, a riot of parrots tied together in a miniskirt and denim jacket. Looks like a woman, sounds like a birdhouse, smells like the contents of a Macy's fragrance counter. He tells her to piss off and tries leaving her in traffic. She sticks to him like a grudge. They are both plastered, for entirely different reasons.

*

They said they'd done everything they could, but they didn't do jack, just stopped the bleeding, slapped on a few bandages, shoved a tube down her throat. They said it's up to Sammy if she lives or dies now. She has to want it, fight for it. This is their way of absolving themselves, but there's nothing you can fucking do about it. When the nurses make their rounds, they make them quietly, quickly, and it feels less like a checkup and more like a check-off: clinical, procedural. Right now you are the only person who can help Sammy, and you don't even know how.

You don't.

*

He shuts out her words and her grasping hands, shuts himself into his own strange crusade, thinks about points and lines and time. He finds a bar he hasn't pissed off yet and asks for the nastiest thing the bartender can make. Carla has not taken the hint—less a hint, more a blatant order—and hooks herself to his belt loop, talks Prada at him.

*

The pall of death has settled against her skin, and she is cold (and cold and colder). You wonder if this is how young people die, violent and abrupt and wrong. You don't know; your parents died sick and old and slow. You and Sammy had clasped warm, dark hands together at their deathbeds, at their funerals, and now you're thinking about funerals, but she's not dead. She's not dead.

Some douche calls after Carla's ass and Denver knocks one of his molars out. They are kicked out of this bar too, and Carla is torn between pleased and puzzled. She oscillates from one to the other while Denver looks for someone else to fight, for points and lines, for some kind of passing sign.

*

Sammy isn't dead yet when they come for you. (That they come at all is a dull surprise.) She hasn't woken up yet, but she isn't dead. You want to ignore them, you want them to go away, but they tell you it's important, it's about Sammy, about what happened when you ditched your little sister for a date and a bar crawl. You get up. forbid Sammy from dying before you get back, and follow the badges down the hall where they're not bothered by the feeble reminder of Sammy's mortality, stumbling and stuttering.

*

He tries telling Carla to fuck off, go home, but she is a leech, deaf to his mindless chants. She's glued to his side, half holding him up, half dragging him back, leading him down familiar streets he doesn't want to be led down. Long dark legs down long dark streets.

*

You watch their shoes (heels lift and settle, polished black leather flashes in hospital lighting) as they give you the rundown, the basics. They outline what happened for you, and you can't feel it. They talk about witnesses and statements and ECPs. Their shoes mutter impatience and boredom. Your shoes sigh in frustration, your jaw clenches over all the words that would change the body into the hall into a girl (two weeks from twenty-three, a year and five months from graduating with a bachelors in molecular biology, prefers dogs over cats, lasagna over spaghetti, smoking over drinking, parents deceased, one older brother, still alive. You're still alive. You're still alive, and it's wrong.)

They use words you've only joked about, words you've used in frustration and false bravado with friends, empty and meaningless and now they're loaded and gunning for you; every use comes back and slides into your skin, sharp and stinging. Everything you've ever laughed at is haunting you from a hospital bed, and you know this is your fault. You think about grudges, about dinner plans canceled for booze runs, about long dark legs and slender fingers, about stupid spats and the lonely sound of dial tones.

*

Your head is clicking into a foreign place, far removed, but infinitely more inviting than right here, right now.

*

The batting cages are dark and empty and Marcus lets him—them—in despite how drunk he—they—is—are. Denver, for one strange moment, thinks Marcus knows and hates him for it, for his understanding, for his unexpected omniscience, for his quiet solidarity.

Carla's smart enough to stay the hell out of the cage but not enough to clear the fence; she hooks painted nails through metal links and presses her face against the cold mesh. She's stopped talking about Gucci or Fiore and started crying, started talking about her couch. He can't figure out why. He just wants her to fucking go home—because he has no home anymore.

*

This is procedure; this is cursory. There's no fire behind these words they bandy around, there's no purpose or plan. This is paper to them; this is personal to you. You study the sketch, burn lines and points into your brain. You won't remember the detectives, but you'll sure as fuck remember the face on that paper.

*

The bat is aluminum and has a satisfying balance in the swing. The weight feels like providence in his hands. He smiles for the first time that night, but it's thin, predatory, and behind it he grits teeth against grief. He runs out of money, and the pitching machine runs out of time. Carla has disappeared, but he doesn't notice. When he leaves the cage he doesn't really feel any better.

Marcus eyes the bat still in Denver's hands, says nothing.

*

The rough sketch is no one you know; the badges shrug and tuck it away, and you want to stop them, you want to ask for that sketch, but your teeth stick to your cheeks, mouth sealed shut. You return to your self-designated station, and they evaporate like they were never really there (because they never really were). Specters and background noise. Nothing feels right anymore.

*

He finds a car, imagines who drives it, and smashes in the windshield. Thinks of pale skin and a ratty red jacket and obliterates the side view mirrors. Thinks of dark blue eyes and caves in the body.

*

Sammy wake up. Until your voice is dry and dusty, until you can't even whisper it because you are a stalwart desert, without reprieve (don't stop), without rain (don't stop), without any plan (don't die). You never should have been so angry. Sammy wake up. You should have showed up anyway and borne her presence in grudging silence. Sammy wake up. She was right anyway, you just didn't want to see it (but you don't want to see this even more).

Sammy wake up, wake up, wake up, a custom fit mantra whirled around like a holy word and a holy war in your empty head.

*

Denver has moved down the line, his bat twisted aluminum. Carla is back, and fuck, she either sobered up or was never as drunk as she said she was. Tennis shoes and jeans and a sweater he recognizes, vaguely, as his. Carla tries pressing a cardboard cup of lukewarm coffee into his hand, wondering how the hell he hasn't gotten arrested yet. And he thinks, they better fucking not. He smashes in another window and thinks they better stay the hell away, those useless fucking badges.

*

You wonder if you hadn't been such a child, would this have ever happened.

(You think about all the apologies you'll make when she wakes up. Because she's not.)

*

A small group of stragglers are pushed from a club that's winding down and closing up. He sees a flash of red in them. This is it. This is him. Points and lines, space and time; a scraggy layer of facial fuzz, short cropped dark hair, wide-set eyes, is that a scar or a laugh line. Carla is his higher self, jabbering nonsense in his ear, nonsense he doesn't want to hear.

HEY. HEY YOU. Is he a man or a mountain, is he shaking or is he shouting. They pull back and look around, buzzed and curious who's yelling. YEAH, YOU. WHITE MOTHERFUCKER. He points at them with gnarled metal. They get one good look at his bat, flashing and dented, and scatter. Carla grabs his arm and yanks it down and he crumples with it because he's fucking tired, he's fucking useless, he's—

Carla curls around him, quiet now, and warm. Soft and safe. She took off her melted wax face some time ago, and Denver realizes that she looks like his sister, battered and raw, a dirty reminder of his flaws and his failures and his treacherous familial infidelity, and he fucking hates her.

He fucking. Hates her.

*

Dead. There's nothing you can do. She flatlines, and those skittish nurses explode into the room like shy birds driven into a cage. They pump her with electricity and abuse her already frail and failing body, and Sammy won't wake up. Sammy will never wake up, and you wonder what the hell was the last thing you even said to her. Did you text her. Did you call her. When you told her she was a nosy bitch, that you can fraternize with whoever the fuck you want, did you second-guess yourself. Did you feel bad at all. Did you even say anything to her, a heads-up on your selfish change of plans, or did you leave her there, a victim waiting for a crime. You are expelled from the room, forced into the hallway, where you stare at passing faces, stark and bright against the backdrop fog of your bomb-shocked brain, and you have nowhere to go from here.

So you do the only thing you know how to do. You hit the bars, and that's where Carla finds you. Three hours later, you are throwing her purse off an overpass.

I Killed a Bird Today

Caitlin Pegar

It was a small bird, a type of finch most likely. My cat pranced through the doggie door and paraded through the house, showcasing his prey thrashing between clenched teeth. Lucky hadn't been feeling well, his old bones catching up to him, and he had been unable to make even the shortest leap up onto the desk chair for the whole week prior. Despite the obvious pain of his captive, I couldn't help but be proud, cooing my congratulations and scritching Lucky's fluffy grey head.

Alex, my brother, held Lucky's head down, forcing him to release it; we didn't want a tiny corpse in our house. It flew on two broken wings and missing tail feathers, up and forward. Blinded by panic, it ricocheted against the wall and fell ten feet away, landing on the side table.

I moved to pick it up, stopped a few inches away. Moved forward again, stopped. Wondered if I should get a towel or a napkin to hold it as I would a dead spider. But it was alive, neither bleeding nor moving, just heaving in shock.

"You got him, Cait?"

I cupped him in my hands as though he were water, his feathers soft in my palm. I held him for a moment, neither of us moving. Shifting him to one hand, he didn't flinch as I pet him crest to back with the tips of my fingers, memorizing the feel of his fur-feathered head, noting the resistance of his skull, and questioning how much force Lucky had to use to break him. Murmuring pleasantries in a language foreign to birds, hoping the cadence of my voice would be enough to soothe him back to perfect health. Feeling not so much his pulse as the speeding rhythm of adrenaline. He blinked at me.

Should I put him down? Should I put him down*? Where? I know how a cat snaps a neck, as Lucky should have.* My mind ghosted through the movements my wrists would take, even knowing I didn't have that courage. *Should I keep him, take him to the vet? Is this fatal? Can I heal him? I couldn't hurt him more. Could I?*

"He's going to die anyway. He'll probably have a heart attack."

I wasn't so sure. Alex didn't see him up close like I did. Didn't come to check on him.

I laid him outside, half hidden under a bush, and brought Lucky to him. I urged him to finish his prey, finish what he'd started. He cleaned his paws and walked away to take a nap. The little bird was too still for him to care now.

I walked away, had to; I would be late to class otherwise.

The bird blinked at me.

I got in my car, backed up, and drove away, watching the bush and realizing I didn't hide him as well as I should have.

~

He couldn't be separated from my mind. I danced with his wings controlling my arms, felt him as space moving around me. I walked paths he may have flown, glanced at trees he could have lived in. I drew him in the margins of notes on Chinese Traditionalism, dreaming of nests and altars. I sat on the hood of my Chevy Cavalier and smoked to calm my nerves, letting the smell of him and tobacco permeate my clothes.

~

Seven hours later, I glanced under the bush, saw nothing, retreated to the house, and looked out the window and saw a man racing down the street. Bald, white shirt, worn-out sneakers. Trying to flee, he was quickly caught by two people, hunters the same size as their prey. They shoved him up against the passenger door of my car. My family heard the commotion and slowly everyone floated to the living room, all five faces peering out the window to watch the scene unfold.

"I should tell them to get off our lawn, go wrestle somewhere else."

"They'll leave. It'll be fine."

"Should we call the cops?"

The hunters looked alike, and the age difference suggested they were a father-daughter team in whatever they were doing. Broad, heavyset adults. Although the same size, the bald man looked smaller against the two of them. Both had a holster; the bald man was unarmed.

"No, someone else will do it."

"Are they kidnapping him?"

"No, they're arresting him."

"I don't see any badges. Or uniforms."

"Maybe it's the Russian mob."

"Should we call the cops?"

The bald man struggled in their grip, the daughter attempting to cuff him. He got a lucky hit and escaped, flying ten feet before tripping and falling on our lawn. The father immediately tackled him, pinning him to the ground. They wrestled, but the bald man never came close to winning.

"No, they're bounty hunters."

"Gambling debts to the mob, probably."

"No, he just skipped out on bail, flew court. Happens all the time."

"Car's been here a while. They've been waiting for him. Probably lured him out."

"Oh look, the neighbors are questioning them."

"See, they've got a book. Bounty hunters."

"They could be lying. Easy to fake."

"If they were kidnapping him, they'd have driven off by now."

"Would they? 'Cause I'd pretend to be a bounty hunter."

"Should we call the cops?"

They got him in cuffs, while neighbors gathered at a respectable distance. The corner neighbors, who lived a hundred or so feet from us, whom we knew about as well as the strangers fighting in front of us, approached them. The daughter brought out a handbook from their black lookout van, flipped to a page, pointed something out. The father manhandled the bald stranger into the back of the van. The man wasn't bleeding or wounded, just cuffed and exhausted, his face more disappointed and ashamed than angry. The father slammed the door shut and got into the driver's seat. The daughter finished her spiel, tromped off our lawn, and joined her father.

"They're ruining our lawn."

They drove away, the crowd of neighbors meandering back to their homes. My family and I dispersed back to our separate rooms, seemingly forgetting it as soon as the car drove away, the handcuffed man in somebody's custody. The dogs barked on at the commotion. Mom yelled at them to shut up.

I asked about the bird.

"Lucky went over and played with it every so often for a couple hours. It was still twitching. Must have lived a long time."

"Oh."

I went outside to see if he was still there. There wasn't even a feather.

There was a smudge on my car window, right where the man's nose and cheek had pressed up against the glass. I'd have to wipe that away later.

Back inside, Lucky jumped in my lap, purring to me.

~

The next day, there was a blood sacrifice. A personal ritual to honor the spirits I didn't save. A familiar motion of pen on paper, filling out forms about my medical history, weight, height, blood pressure, and whether I had taken aspirin the night before. A drink of water to make the blood flow better, a squeeze of the rubber ball to pop my veins, I lay back with a needle in the crook of my elbow, watched the blood fill a bag and four vials, watched the needle slip away, and my arm being bandaged.

After, I whispered to his spirit, "See? I'm sorry."

He didn't whisper back. I didn't expect him to.

928 Romeo

C. Gregory

I was sneaky and I was in love. I was old enough to have a crappy job and some spending money, but young enough to live without sleep. Night after night, I would tiptoe out of the house after calling for a taxi. We lived at the top of a hill, and I would stand on the neighbor's curb and watch for the taxi to appear at the bottom. It never failed to thrill me when I saw the lit taxicab sign round the bend and start to climb. A silent torch of my love, I used to think.

Wasn't I the gallant one? Stealing out at night, risking it all to be with the one I loved until the cruel pressure of sunrise tore us apart again. Of course, we were never really that far from each other since we went to the same high school and lived in the same town. But what an adventure to hire a cab to whisk me to my girlfriend late at night while the world slept, while our parents slept. We were so romantic, so mature. Inevitably, I would break her heart, and in our final moments together she would say, "Pretend you never knew me." I like to believe that some small part of me knew the truth, even back then, that dating girls was only a phase, an earnest attempt at an easier life. But then, I was in love for the first time.

I took this midnight ride so often that the cabbies in the company began to refer to me as "928 Romeo" on their radios. My romantic endeavors had earned me a handle, a combination of my street address and a famous lover. I was proud. I felt dashing climbing into a yellow Crown Vic, the entrance into my own romantic adventure. The wide upholstered bench of the back seat was always mysteriously stained and pocked with cigarette burns, and yet I'd never sat on anything so soft.

Most of the cab drivers were silent and polite, not even slightly interested in their late night fares, but I remember the adultness of them. Their lives were foreign to me, these men who worked graveyard shifts ferrying strangers across the dark city. They knew things I did not know, adult things that went far beyond any R-rated movie. I imagined them shaking their heads softly whenever they got the call to pick me up, mumbling, "Teenage love," as they put the taxi into gear. At four thirty in the morning, in the darkest hours before the impending sunrise, I would slink out of my girlfriend's bedroom and cross a side yard to the street. The cab would be waiting, lights off, engine humming. Sometimes I'd have to tap on the window to wake my cabbie up.

There was one cabbie who, over a matter of weeks, became my regular. He was somewhere in his forties and always on the hunt for a good time. His hair was thin, his face craggy, the kind of face I would now describe as the result of hard living. Back then, he felt like my accomplice, a late night courier of love. We never exchanged names or spoke at length, but he let me sit up front with him and showed me where he hid his porno magazines. He wouldn't object when I would ask him to stop at a liquor store where underage kids could buy cigarettes.

Rolling through the empty, predawn streets, he would share snippets of his romps.

"You know about hookers?"

"Um, yeah. Never been with one, though." I would casually flip through a skin mag.

"Well, usually you get either experience or looks, but sometimes, if you're lucky, you get both."

I nodded as if I knew what he was talking about.

"We got this chick last week; she was hot *and* talented."

"Who's we?"

"Me and some buddies, you know, maybe three or four of us. And let me tell you, she handled us all, no problem—at the same time!"

"Oh, cool." I stared down at the magazine of naked women in my lap, unsure of what "handled" really meant or how a conversation like this is supposed to continue or end.

"Yeah, that's my newest mag. Check out the center. She's shaved."

His was a world I could not comprehend. It was too adult—too too. But it made me feel cool in a way; it rounded out the thrill of those illicit trysts. I didn't know enough to pity or blame him. I hadn't fully developed the grownup tools of judgment or righteous anger. I was getting a glimpse of what felt like a vulgar and uncouth world, and I liked it.

My world was a teenage fever of marathon make out sessions and phone calls late at night that went on until we would both fall asleep, the phone tucked into bed. There was no satiation for us. Necking was as natural as breathing. Every sentence we spoke sounded something like, "I love you, I love you, I love you." I know now that it's foolish to look back and pretend there was only fuzzy young love surrounding us. It's foolish to even regard what happened between us as love at all. As if there weren't greater forces already at work inside me.

But there was a convenience in having this kind of public relationship. It was proof that whatever my true feelings, at least I was having lots of straight sex. The gallantry and adventure added to the theater I was building and made it easy for me to play the part. I could cater to her feelings as much as avoid my own. I believed I had an enlightened sense of love, an evolved love. I thought it very advanced of me to entertain what I thought were unconventional ideas. I told her once that if she ever wanted to sleep with someone else, I would be just fine with it. When other boys would talk to her at school, I took no offense. I thought I was bohemian.

"Who was that?" I would ask.

"Why? Are you jealous?"

"No. I think jealousy is a waste of time. People who get jealous must be insecure or something. I know that I love you and that you love me, no matter what, even if you were attracted to someone else."

"I get jealous if I see you with another girl."

"Well, that doesn't make sense. You know I love you. I would never do anything. I don't even think about other girls."

How magnanimous! I was the perfect boyfriend. I even thought I liked cunnilingus. It wasn't until years later that jealously would blossom in my heart while dating my first boyfriend. Little claws appeared on my fingers at even the thought of him talking to other boys. My jealousy finally spoke the truth.

Back then, I persisted in loving her and reveling in the lust. Whenever we spent the night together, the sex was the way teenage sex should be—breathless, headlong, flushed. My dazed glow would trail me from her bedroom to the taxi, as I could hear my own pulse.

One night, I hopped into the cab and noticed that my cabbie seemed distracted. He made no move to get going but instead tossed one of his special magazines onto my lap. "Hold on a minute. No rush, right?" I agreed with him and opened the magazine, unimpressed by the pictures as I pretended not to care what my cabbie was doing. I played it nonchalant. I played it cool. Besides, I didn't know I could tell an adult what to do.

So I just watched, fearful and uncomprehending, as my cabbie carefully folded a piece of foil into a little trough, sprinkled a white powder into it, and then held his lighter underneath until it started to bubble and smoke. He leaned forward and sucked in the smoke with a cutoff straw, sweeping back and forth over the foil.

"Damn that's good!" he yelled while kicking his head back, letting the little straw fall into his lap. I turned and stared straight ahead. I felt trapped. The sky was turning gray in the east, and I had just watched my cabbie freebase. Of course, back then I didn't know what freebasing was. I didn't know about drugs and drug addicts or the attraction of hairless women and fake boobs. I didn't even know myself.

"Ok, Romeo, let's get you home. You ready?"

I wasn't.

Passion at the Wedding

Caitlin Pegar

the hall was set on fire with the snap of a match and all the guests went wilting while we
went searching searching for whatever imp it was that thought it fun to set the flowers aflame

you ran to me you ran to me across town across the chapel across the hall to tell me
the building was burning you set off the alarm and told me the building was burning

you didn't know that I had done it I didn't tell you that I had done it though the evidence was
there the evidence was there at my feet burning the bones because you ran a little too late

a little too late wouldn't stop the flames I couldn't feel but I screamed because you thought I
should I should but the nerves had been burned so I couldn't feel except for the edge of the skin

so when we ran searching searching for the imp that thought it fun to burn my feet I didn't tell didn't
tell you I needn't scream for it felt as though I was gliding a foot off the ground a trail of fire two feet

off two feet far the fire tailed as we tailed the trail of the imp who must have been cold must
have been as he had given his fire to feet and flowers and hall and the tailed trail had gone cold

we went back to the hall to find it still aflame and the flowers wilting wilting under the heat of the
blaze so we went home leaving feet and flowers and hall to burn out to burn themselves out

but as we tangled in our sheets tangled up the sheets our tango and my feet caught the sheets
aflame you touched your fingers to the blaze because of course you did of course you did

and I wouldn't tell you I won't tell you I met the devil in a coffee shop and she asked me for coffee
and a light so I gave her coffee and a light because of course I did of course I did she was blowing

smoke and I was blowing smoke when I told her she owed me one she did coffee's not cheap
so when I woke to coffee on my table I knew I knew that something you or I would be set ablaze

I didn't tell you so we grabbed cigarettes to light off my flaming feet but after we lit the flames of my
feet fluttered out though the bed kept blazing we huddled for warmth blowing smoke at each other

you wondered if the hall was still ablaze and the flowers still wilting they were nice flowers they'll be
nice ashes though not allowed though not aloud I wondered to me or to her do you now owe a light

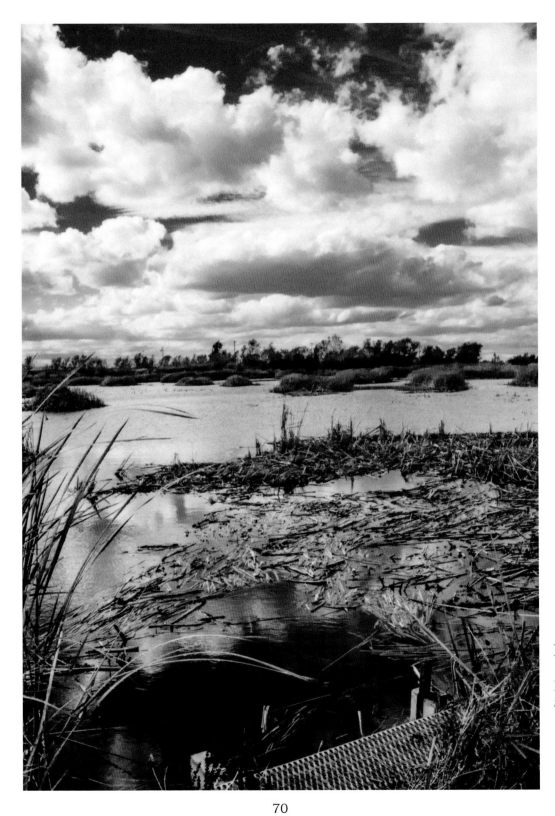

Kyle Doka
Untitled
Ink Jet Print
8x10 Inches

American Sentences

(composed during a storm)

Stuart L. Canton

The clouds loom overhead with broad, gray fuselages about to burst.

Streaks of sunlight shine through a marbled ceiling of slate sky and black cloud.

Mi abuelita calls the crowded noise of perched sparrows, "rain chatter."

White blossoms billow and blow away on the wind that carries the clouds.

Newspapers and pamphlets flap silently in the shadow of thunder.

Hanging chimes are instruments set out for the wind's eager hands to play.

Concrete walls darken when wet, with ash shades seemingly sketched with charcoal.

Stairs change into pools swollen with rain, crumpled leaves, and cigarette butts.

Snails attempt the ten yards from one side of the walkway to the other.

Shoes squelch in dark puddles of cold water that seeps into socks, wets feet.

Early darkness brings the soggy glow of street lamps to the evening.

The twisted fingers of a tree hold its last few leaves to the gray sky.

Distinguished Author
Julia B. Levine

is the winner of numerous awards for her work, including the 2003 Tampa Review Prize for her second full-length collection, *Ask;* the 1998 Anhinga Poetry Prize and bronze medal from *Fore-Word* magazine for her first collection, *Practicing for Heaven;* and a Discovery/The Nation award. Her latest poetry collection, *Small Disasters Seen in Sunlight,* inaugurates a new poetry series for Louisiana State University Press. Her work appears in several new anthologies, including *The Places That Inhabit Us, The Autumn House Anthology of Contemporary American Poetry*, and *The Bloomsbury Anthology of Contemporary Jewish American Poetry*. She holds a PhD from UC Berkeley and lives and works in Davis, California.

Suicide Triptych

1.

It is strange enough to wake inside the gleam of it,
three boys carrying bouquets of forget-me-nots across a field,

is to come upon a terrible brightness, a bridal, raw joy.
Was it your heart? I ask, confused. Or not.

Either a great loneliness invited you into my dream
or I am partly somewhere else, the flowering pear trees

collapsing into a ferocious snow of blossoms, a door
flung back, a white hallway opening over the street.

Yes, my heart, you answer, pulling me closer
into the poorly healed places between us.

2.

No, I said when the nurse asked if I wanted to see your body.
As in what travels out of otherness—

car keys, REI card, black marble painted with our galaxy
falling through the other side of sky.

As in where we go in memory when something lost
turns back with news of the next world

cut out. No I did not want to be half-
carried into the grieving room, one cot

with no one there. A privacy. A white absence
at the end. As in the idea of soul

unlatched from matter and nothing to be done.
A dirge in diminishing intervals. Nothing

talking softly in its sleep.

3.

But when I stop my car to stare at the flowering,
there is a widening vex and truth

undressed, I think, from your name.

So then, who am I talking to?
The field's annunciation, the oak's dictum?

The morphine of this almond orchard in bloom?

Listen,
because the damaged world interrupts its own sadness

with spring's fleshy jazz, I can believe in death
as the ashes we threw into wind,

and you, as what slipped through

the unthinkable pressure that being endures.
That needs you

the way the dark branches need each bud,
enveloped in light, to be summoned briefly

here, in order to break.

73

Letter to My Left Eye

To you alone, and not your partner
blackening past sweetness, right retina bled and scarred

and the world mostly gone. Edges yes,
the green lift and fall of live oaks,

something accidental and metal wheeling past,
but for every detail alive and embodied in its sensed presence—

the red of unripe berries darkening on a vine,
daylilies parting their buttered lobes to heat—

now it's entirely up to you.
You that gives me a warbler at morning

impossibly perched on the pool,
each bone like a tiny piccolo playing wind.

You that calls the horses to the edge of summer,
their tails twitching like seeded grass, saddled and riding light.

And you alone that trues the line of the reeds
and the pond as it suddenly quivers,

then splinters into rain. Oh,
loyal and devoted window out of the mind's torment,

let this be an ode to how I'm touched
from every corner of the hour by you.

Let me praise your endurance
even as I curse the body's tryst with twinning,

knowing that one might leave the other,
might drive to the top of the tallest building in town

and jump.
Let me ask too, which of you opened the door last night

to my dead friend, coming as he did to me
in a dream, all dressed in white?

There was a stain like old blood or berry juice on my skirt.
I kept touching it, the imperfection,

feeling for once that it did not need to be erased.
Like the musician writing that he loved beautiful melodies

about terrible things,
it has never been easy to see things as they truly are.

So let this epistolary become the first of many prayers
about starting over with what burns or wanders lost

or cuts with a rawness carried in the pockets of our deepest name.
And remind her, will you, our traitor

asleep in a roomlight of solitude,
about joy and loss, grief and desire.

How they have always lived together. That as soon as one closes,
the other opens even wider.

Acacia Trees

And if it matters now that your parents beat you
when you were young, cursing your name, their God,

it is only in the startled way you walk these hills
after rain, past the razored shine of a waterfall

plunging over rock, into sea.
You say you have lost enough to look behind.

You say you are almost blind, and so you see it differently,
at the beginning of your father's dying,

when he could walk, could still stand
with your mother at the museum, before a photo

of a boarded-up building titled *House of Dreams.*
Though you never understood what it meant

until now, to carry someone long enough
to be carried back out. To turn willingly, tenderly

towards the idea of an old man and woman
holding hands and weeping, heads bowed so low,

their past retires into the kind of beauty that arrives
after torment. That glistens like moths

brushing through these reeds. That sighs
like this sudden temple of acacia trees

collapsed into ground, an entire grove of flowering thorn
so flush with a feathery, yellow bloom,

the storm's savage generosity of wind and rain
must have laid the giant canopies down to dirt,

must have broken a wild sanctuary
out of the weight of its own blossoming.

Dear Carol Wald,

I remember you insisted the sunroom
had the only decent light
in which to paint my little sister,
as she leant against the chair
where I sat in a red crepe skirt.
Head down, my two hands cupped the dark lump
of Lord Raisin, my guinea pig, in my lap.
On the other side, my little brother
opened his mitt like a brown flower
and stared. Enormous,
that canvas and its searing yellow ground,
the floor sketched as a floating line,
a fuse burning itself out.
In the two weeks you lived with us—
long enough, you said,
to understand your subjects—
I never remember talking to you,
just sitting silently,
waiting for it to be over.
Now, nearly a half-century later,
your painting tossed in the dumpster
after my father died, my mother unwilling
to hang it in her new apartment,
I've wanted to thank you countless times
for the cryptic power of art.
How you lent me a window
where the dark shapes turned and turned
but did not turn away. Year after year
I lay on the living room carpet
and studied those three kids,
wanting to ask how a picture
could hold what hadn't yet happened.
If you knew, even then,
what couldn't be saved.

The Night My Husband Comes Home
from the Hospital

The earth shakes us awake, shudders the sea,
throws cases of wine across the valley's floor.

Still, it is a kind of singing—
the nakedness of terror beside the trillium,

moths batting up against the petalled canticles,
sirens changing the night's silence in wind.

Easy to forget how thin a crust
the quotidian spreads over such restlessness.

Easy to believe a scarecrow stands in the future,
beneath a torrent of gulls

tearing our overcoat of hours apart. Forgive me
if I've forgotten how to live inside a singular body—

even the bishop pines lean on sky,
the bluffs clip their enormity to a silver net of vines.

Eventually the waves will settle,
the lash and spin of buoys slow. Until then,

forgive me if I've forgotten everything
except the sunken blocks tethered to each float—

dead weight of one
pulling against the risk of the other

as it nods to a dark and beautiful whole.

Interview with Julia B. Levine
October 2014

American River Review: Please describe yourself in one word and tell us how that vision of yourself affects your writing.

Julia Levine: Honest. This gets me in trouble all the time, but it is something I am not willing to part with, especially in my writing. And let me emphasize the important difference between fact and truth. I'm not a lawyer or politician. Not only would I likely fail at either endeavor, I am driven by my need to understand what lies underneath the facts of our experience and what then can be brought to light in its contradictory, complex, essential form.

ARR: Is there anything you are afraid to write about? Why or why not?

JL: No. There are subjects, though, that still feel too complex for me to write about in any honest or original way. But of course, with distance and age, all my failed attempts seem to lead me a bit closer. And this is all I ever wanted from poetry—a chance to come closer to some elusive, complex truth that surprises me.

ARR: How has anything that terrified you as a child carried over into your poetry as an adult?

JL: Both the terror and vivid aliveness of childhood are archetypal elements; this is what I believe, along with genetic inheritance, makes up the ground of our particular, unique selves. And because poetry is often a working out of experience into truth and voice, there is no way not to be influenced by these earliest experiences. By that I don't mean simply the content of our work; I mean our own unique syntax, and how and where we hear silence and music in language, and where in a poem we leave, and how we choose to return.

ARR: How has anything comforting to you as a child carried over into your poetry as an adult?

JL: I'm not sure how to answer this question except to say that likely what saved me from my childhood was fantasy. And that included, first and foremost, hours and days of imaginative play, books, art, religion, music. Fantasy was how I escaped when circumstances were cruel.

ARR: What idea upsets you more: believing in a piece you've written that is considered a critical failure, or dashing off something that feels inconsequential only to have it be a commercial or critical success? Why?

JL: This is a funny question for me because I have never written with publication in mind. In fact, a loyal friend sent my first manuscript off to contests because I wouldn't. When it was published, I had no idea what the judges had seen! I'm terrible about sending things out. That's why I love someone like you asks for me to send them poems. With a few exceptions, almost all of my work has been published in this way.

ARR: You tie your poems to particular places. How do the places you've lived in or visited influence your writing?

JL: *I have a chronic vision condition that has always made it hard for me to see, and so I have a relatively synesthetic experience of every place I have ever lived in or been. This is how I experience myself in the world. I can't seem to write about anything without writing about place.*

ARR: When your poems bare such personal situations and emotions, what are the special issues that come into play in the revision process?

JL: *I really don't want to hurt anyone. I remember when my father was dying. I wanted to dedicate my next book to him before he was gone; I confessed that I was worried that my view of the truth would hurt him. To my astonishment, he replied that I shouldn't worry about that because it was mine, not his. In essence, this was permission to have my own voice, and it was a blessing to have him say that before he died.*

But to get back to your question, I have struggled with this, especially in persona poems. The truth is, though, that poetry is fiction, not memoir, not non fiction. The poet needs to revise and change facts to reach truth. The reader needs to remember that.

ARR: How do you balance vocation, avocation, social life, and family? How do they overlap?

JL: *This is a hard one. I often wish I didn't have to work at my vocation and could just write. My parents were very unsupportive of my wish to be a writer, and I let that influence me to a large degree. However, on the other hand, I think my vocation was a similar working out of early experiences (as is my avocation) so that I could have the conscious, complicated life I have now. When I die, I think the writing will not matter as much as the fact that I learned how to love well. This has everything to do with my vocation, and perhaps, most of all, with the family that my husband and I have created. Social life—that is the dessert—and I love dessert!! I think my social life suffers the most because of the writer's need for solitude as well as the juggling act between so many competing demands. But oh well . . .*

ARR: Are your poems emotionally challenging for you to read aloud?

JL: *Yes, some of them are. And so sometimes I don't. I have poems that were published in my books or journals that I have never read aloud. That can change though, depending on the audience or the event.*

ARR: Your images using the word "snow" are quite lovely. What special significance does snow have for you?

JL: *I love that you asked me that. I never thought about it, but I grew up primarily in Michigan where it snowed a lot! And my family was from Québec, so we often traveled by train or car up to these vast, white landscapes. When I think on this question, I realize that my love of silence in poetry and music is often akin to my feeling of snow as quieting the noise of the landscape. Snow seems to blanket, as in cloak or protect, the world, but at the same time, something essential is revealed. Snow, also for me, was an entry point into a sense of being between places, those spaces, like dreams, that are and are not of this world. Waking up to the first snow in winter was like that—I am now in a world that is and is not the one I left behind last night when I fell asleep.*

Literature Staff

Editorial

Faculty Adviser
Michael Spurgeon

Editors-in-Chief
Bethanie Humphreys (S14, F14)
Joshua Jonas (F13)

Associate Editors-in-Chief
Anique Bailey (F13)
E. Dominguez (S14)
Elizabeth "Betsy" Harper (F14)
Andrey Shamshurin (F14)
Thomas Smith (S14, F14)
Blake Steele (S14)

Publishers
Sherry DeTinne-Cassel (S14)
Elizabeth "Betsy" Harper (S14)
Kenneth Hinton (F14)

Office Managers
Tiffany Bush (F13)
Katia Monterrey (F14)
Alexis Stordahl (S14)

Assistant Office Manager
Katia Monterrey (S14)

Fiction

Managing Editors
E. Dominguez (F13)

Samuel Pinnegar (S14)
Heather Skinkle (F14)

Associate Managing Editors
Samuel Pinnegar (F13)
Andrey Shamshurin (S14)

Genre Editors
Alexis Alexander (S14)
Diva Anwari (F13, S14)
Valorie Castillo (S14)
Chris Chavarria (F13)
Gloria Daskalakis (F13)
Jacob DeSersa (S14)
Elizabeth "Betsy" Harper (F13)
Kenneth Hinton (S14)
Katia Monterrey (S14)
Heather Skinkle (S14)
Thomas Smith (F13)
Alexis Stordahl (S14)

Associate Editors
Stuart Canton (S14)
Jon Escamilla (S14)
Stefanie Kurtz (S14)

Creative Nonfiction

Managing Editors
Jon Escamilla (F14)
Josh Lacy (F13)
Maria Oswalt (S14)

Associate Managing Editors
Matthew Landavazo (S14)
Bryan Roseberry (F13)

Genre Editors
Jon Escamilla (S14)
Stefanie Kurtz (S14)
Matthew Landavazo (F13)
Maria Oswalt (F13)
Thomas Smith (F14)
David Vallejo (S14)
Diana Vo (F13)

Associate Editors
Diva Anwari (S14)
Valorie Castillo (S14)
Elaine Lenore (S14)
Kourtney Hollomon (S14)
Andrey Shamshurin (S14)

Poetry

Managing Editors
Christopher Chavarria (S14, F14)
Madeline Gerlach (F13)

Associate Managing Editors
Madeline Gerlach (S14)
Blake Steele (F13)

Genre Editors
Stuart Canton (S14)
Elaine Lenore (S14)
John Hill (F13)
Kourtney Hollomon (F13, S14)
Bethanie Humphreys (F13)
Velvet Sharon McKenzie (F13)
Amanda Ochoa (F13)
Caitlin Pegar (F13)
Darrell Parker (S14, F14)

Associate Editors
Alexis Alexander (S14)
Jacob DeSersa (S14)

Copy Editors
Stephen Abel (F14)
Jessica "Jesse" Armstrong (F14)
Tammy Ballard (F14)
Jarom Briggs (F14)
Sherry DeTinne-Cassel (F14)
Isabel Geerer (F14)
Courtney Klousner (F14)
Ivalyn "Ivy" McDonald (F14)
Rosina Miranda (F14)
Saleem Obeidat (F14)
Micah Rankin (F14)

Reading Directors
Sherry DeTinne-Cassel (F14)
Bethanie Humphreys (F14)
Katia Monterrey (F14)

Contributors Page Editors
Stephen Abel (F14)
Courtney Klousner (F14)
Rosina Miranda (F14)
Micah Rankin (F14)
Heather Skinkle (F14)

Patrons Page Editors
Jessica "Jesse" Armstrong (F14)
Matthew Landavazo (S14)

Staff Page Editors
Isabel Geerer (F14)
Ivalyn "Ivy" McDonald (F14)
Saleem Obeidat (F14)
Andrey Shamshurin (F14)
David Vallejo (S14)

Acknowledgements Page Editors
Tammy Ballard (F14)
Jarom Briggs (F14)
Christopher Chavarria (F14)

Awards Page Editors
Jacob DeSersa (F14)
Jon Escamilla (F14)

Distinguished Author Liaison
Elizabeth "Betsy" Harper (F14)

Marketing Directors
Kenneth Hinton (F14)
Heather Skinkle (S14)

Special Projects Manager
Velvet Sharon McKenzie (S14)

Communications Directors
Darrell Parker (F14)
Thomas Smith (F14)
Micah Rankin (F14)

Literature Contributors

Anique Bailey was born in Santa Clara County, raised in Humboldt County, and currently resides in Sacramento. She has made only cursory forays over the state line, with the farthest destination being Nevada. She is an Anthropology major at American River College and this is her second time being published in the *American River Review*.

Tiffany Bush currently resides in Antelope, California. She is pursuing a career as a novelist, which her cats attempt, in vain, to sabotage. Tiffany served four semesters on the *American River Review* as the filing cabinet-obsessed office manager. This is her first publication, but it's far from her last. Her piece is dedicated to the memory of Doris Albrecht, Grandmother Extraordinaire, who passed away in July 2014.

Stuart L. Canton lives in Sacramento, California, where he has been published in many local poetry publications. He has been featured at the Sacramento Poetry Center and Sacramento's longest running poetry series, Joe Montoya's Poetry Unplugged, at Luna's Cafe. Stuart was first encouraged to share his writing with publishers while studying at American River College, where he recently earned an AA in English. He is now studying literature at CSU, Sacramento, where he is continuing to develop his voice and his writer's toolbox. This is his first time being published in the *American River Review*.

Carlitta Cole-Kelly spent her childhood on the Mississippi Gulf Coast with both sets of grandparents, later relocating to New Jersey and Hawaii in her teen years. She is a craft artist and writer of short stories, devotionals, poems, and articles. She has been published in the *UND Alumni Review* and *Gospel Roads* magazines, and has a BAS in nursing from CSU, Bakersfield. After 25-plus years of caring for others, she is finally pursuing her passion for writing by taking creative non-fiction and digital design classes at American River College to prepare for her "next career."

E. Dominguez was the only kid growing up in the San Francisco Bay Area that dreamed of living with her grandmother in Sacramento. Ed attended American River College to do "something other than writing," and ended up on the staff of the 2014 *American River Review* anyway. With a literary publishing certificate in one hand and the other reaching for an AA, Ed is working on one too many things from video games to movie scripts to creative non-fiction novels, and hopes to someday be known as That Person Who Writes Good Stuff.

Rachel Gardner is working on revising her first novella, a noir detective piece set in a post-apocalyptic Lovecraftian dystopia. This is her fifth time being published in the *American River Review*.

Isabel Geerer lives in North Highlands, California and is currently working for the non-profit organization 916 Ink as a Wordslinger, where she teaches creative writing to children from fourth to twelfth grade. She also works for Adventure Club Before and After School Care where she plays games and reads books with

the kids. She has earned an AA and an Associate Teacher's Permit from American River College. She has served on the staff of the *American River Review* as managing poetry editor and twice as associate editor-in-chief. Isabel has published poetry in the *American River Review*, *The Gap-Toothed Madness*, and *Tule Review*, and is currently working on a young adult novel. She hopes to promote children's literacy in as many ways as possible.

C. Gregory was born and raised on the beaches of Los Angeles. After a decade living further north, he now resides in Sacramento where he longs for coastal fog and continually attempts to wrangle his thoughts onto paper. A lover of short stories, he hopes to publish his own collection one day and finally say something true.

Kourtney Holloman was born and raised in Citrus Heights, California, where she still resides. She is a former poetry genre editor of the *American River Review* and a proud graduate of American River College. She has AAs in English, liberal arts, and social science. Kourtney still enjoys taking classes at American River College. She plans to transfer to CSU, Sacramento in the Fall of 2015, where her goal is to receive her BA in English with an emphasis in creative writing. Kourtney believes that all facets of writing are simply ways in which we can unlock a better understanding of ourselves and the nature of the human psyche.

Bethanie Humphreys lives in Citrus Heights, California, and is a published poet and mixed media visual artist. Her poetry has appeared in *Late Peaches*, *Tule Review*, *The Gap-Toothed Madness*, *Sacramento Voices II*, and the 2014 *American River Review*, and she also had a poem performed in the *River City Anthology* at Wilkerson Theater. Her artwork has been shown in multiple venues, was chosen as curator's pick for Sac Open Studios 2014, and was featured by Sacramento Bee's Victoria Dalkey as one of the "top five picks for exhibits to fuel the imagination" in February, 2013. Bethanie earned a BA in Spanish from CSU, Sacramento, an AA in behavioral science from Modesto Junior College, and a literary publishing certificate from American River College. Her goal is to further the cross-pollinization of the literary and visual arts.

Austin Ice lives in Sacramento, California. He graduated with high honors from American River College, where he was a co-writer for the honors program and honors club bylaws. He would like to use the writing experience he has gained from his classes at ARC and CSU, Sacramento as fuel to finish and publish his novel.

Elaine Lenore lives in her hometown of Sacramento, and served as an associate poetry editor for the *American River Review*. She has enjoyed attending SummerWords and other creative writing workshops at American River College. She is currently working on a collection of poems as well as a creative nonfiction account of her tempestuous and sometimes ridiculous life.

Michelle Lepori transferred to the University of New Orleans from American River College. Her favorite memories of ARC include Figure Fridays with the Art Club and learning inside the James Kaneko Gallery. She continues to focus on the craft of writing, the technique of art, and the world as a stage.

Diane McCarthy is the author of the novel, *The Spirit of the River*, and as DianeMmm, the young adult novel, *The Bully Room*. At American River College, she is exploring the art new media courses that enable writers to design and publish their own work. She lives in El Dorado Hills.

Velvet Sharon McKenzie is a Nevada City, California native who moved to Sacramento to study English and plans to earn a PhD in American Literature. Velvet worked as the editor-in-chief of the 2014 *American River Review*. She also works as a professional editor and journalist for the local trauma medical industry where she specializes in human interest stories from the perspective of victims of serious trauma, but her true interest lies in writing screenplays about people who are victims of themselves. Velvet had two poems published in the 2014 *American River Review*, one of which won first place in the Columbia Scholastic Press Association's Gold Circle Awards for Student Work, Formal Poetry category.

Eric Orosco is a California transplant living in Moscow, Idaho. During his brief attendance at American River College, he served as fiction editor for the 2013 *American River Review*. Eric's goals in writing are rooted in the idea that good fiction attempts to answer a question. After completing his BA in English, Eric plans to attend a master of fine arts program in fiction. Currently he is serving as editor-in-chief for the University of Idaho's upcoming undergraduate literary magazine, *Vandalism*, where he is able to apply the skills and knowledge he acquired while working on the staff of the *American River Review*.

Caitlin Pegar hails from Sacramento, California, and is currently studying for her degree in veterinary science. A former staff member and contributing writer of the *American River Review*, she writes to share and explore experiences. She aims to publish her stories, poetry, and artwork while continuing to help animals.

Blake Steele lives in Sacramento, California. He has served three semesters on the staff of the *American River Review* and ultimately aspires to write stories and poems that people take too seriously.

Patrons

Nobel - $1000+

American River College Associated Student Body Student Senate

Office of the Vice President of Instruction

Pulitzer - $500+

Dr. Thomas Greene

English Area

Bestseller - $250+

Tammy Montgomery

Rod Siegfried

First Edition - $100+

Lois Ann Abraham and Thomas O'Toole

John Bell

Kirsten Corbin

Robert Frew

Kenneth Hinton

Dr. Lucille Rybka

Holden and Catherine Spurgeon

First Chapter - $50+

Chris and John Hess

David Merson

Shannon Pries

Pamela and Harold Schneider

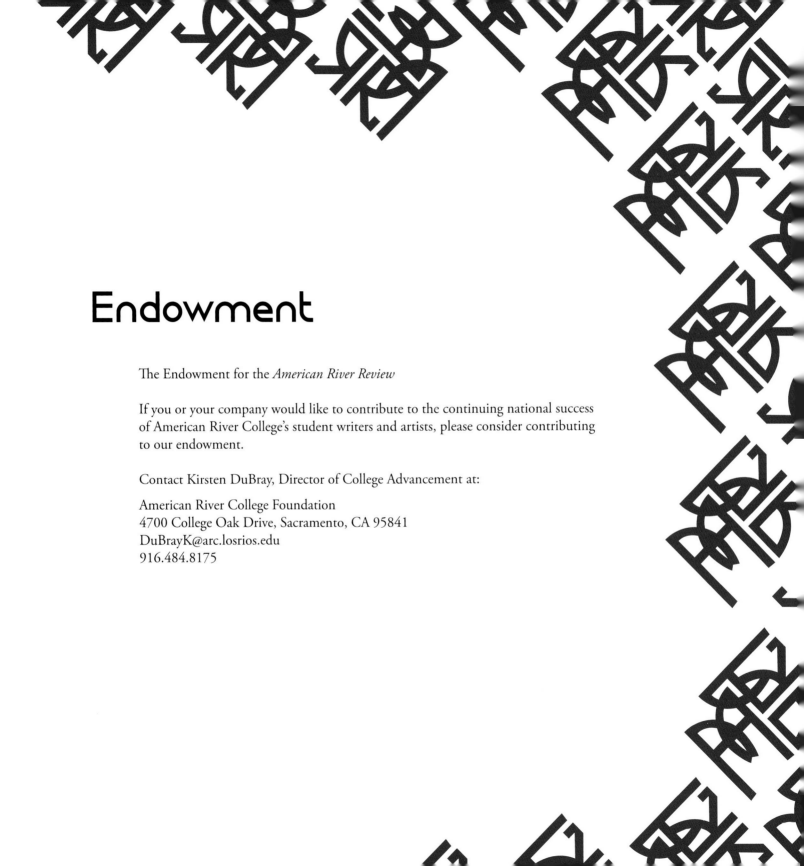

Endowment

The Endowment for the *American River Review*

If you or your company would like to contribute to the continuing national success of American River College's student writers and artists, please consider contributing to our endowment.

Contact Kirsten DuBray, Director of College Advancement at:

American River College Foundation
4700 College Oak Drive, Sacramento, CA 95841
DuBrayK@arc.losrios.edu
916.484.8175

Art Selection Process

The Art Selection class meets every spring. Over the course of three days in February, hundreds of students submit paintings, sculptures, photographs, comic art, 3D designs, and digital art that are then photographed by professional photographers at American River College's Kaneko Gallery. The class then discusses every single piece extensively and debates its merit before putting it to a final vote. The selected pieces make up the gallery on these pages.

Every fall, the Art New Media College Magazine Design and Production class meets. The class is organized into four teams: design, production, fashion, and gallery. The teams work together to prepare the art selections for print, layout the art gallery, the fashion section, and design the overall magazine.

American River Review

Literature Selection Process

In an eighteen-month process, student literature is submitted, read, selected, and revised. Every semester, hundreds of pieces of poetry, fiction, nonfiction, and alternative genre are submitted for consideration to the College Literary Magazine class. Every submission is read, and the discussion of a single piece can last an entire class session. A final vote decides which works will be selected, edited, and published. The staff meets with the authors of the selected pieces to discuss the work and offer feedback for the author's consideration, with the goal of helping each piece reach its highest potential.

Students of American River College and participants in SummerWords: The American River College Creative Writing Colloquium are eligible to submit.

All words, images, and designs appearing in this magazine, as well as the production arrangements and editing of stories and poems, are the products of American River College students.

All ideas and opinions expressed in the magazine are the sole expression of student artists and do not reflect the ideas or opinions of our staff, American River College, the Los Rios Community College District, its employees, or its trustees. All brands, corporations, product names, and other references contained herein are trademarks, registered trademarks, or trade names of their respective holders. All literature and image copyrights are held by their respective owners.

American River College
4700 College Oak Drive
Sacramento, CA, 95841
www.americanriverreview.com
AmericanRiverReview@gmail.com

Acknowledgments

The staff of the 2015 *American River Review* would like to thank the following people, as without their support, assistance, and inspiration, this publication would not be possible:

Interim Presidents Marie Smith, Bill Karns, and Pam Walker; President Thomas Greene; Vice President of Instruction Colleen Owings;

Included in the prologue is an excerpt from THE DIARY OF ANAIS NIN, Volume Three: 1939-1944. Copyright © 1969 by Anais Nin and renewed Rupert Pole and Gunther Stuhlmann. Reprinted by permission of Houghton Mifflin Harcourt Publishing Company. All rights reserved.

Former faculty advisers of the magazine Professors Connie Johnstone, Harold Schneider, David Merson, & Betty Nelsen;

Former Dean of English Area Tammy Montgomery; Interim Dean of English Area Victoria Maryatt;

Dean of Fine and Applied Arts Adam Karp;

Mary Higgins and Shane Lipscomb for their never-ending crisis management;

Chair of the Art New Media Department Matt Stoehr;

English Department Chairs John Bell and Kathleen O'Brien;

Kirsten DuBray and the American River College Foundation;

Bruce Clarke and Jean Kennedy for the art photography;

Professors Bonnie Spencer and Diane Grant-Tuscano for their work in the Fashion Department;

The Horticulture Area for allowing the Fashion Department access for photo shoots;

Mick Sheldon for access to the Kaneko Gallery;

The American River College Bookstore for display and sales;

Marlene Huttner, Art New Media Lab Technician;

Don Reid and everyone at Print Services;

Reyna Spurgeon and Heather Orr Martinez for their love and support;

And most importantly, we would like to acknowledge all the students at American River College who have submitted their work and made the *American River Review* what it is today.

Awards

Associated Collegiate Press
National Pacemaker Award
2006 | 2007 | 2008 | 2010 | 2012 | 2013 | 2014

American Scholastic Press Association
First Place with Special Merit 2007
First Place 2011

College Media Advisers
Best of Show (1st Place)
National College Media Convention 2008

Columbia Scholastic Press Association
First Place Overall Design, Literary for Magazines 2010
Gold Crown Award
2005 | 2006 | 2007 | 2008 | 2009 | 2011

Community College Humanities Association Literary Magazine Competition
Best in Nation
1990 | 1993 | 1995 | 1997 | 1999 | 2008 | 2011 | 2012 | 2013 | 2014

as a concept artist, character designer, or storyboard artist in the creative production of an animated TV show or movie.

Jordan Siangco is a native of Carmichael, California. He has had artwork in multiple shows and is very close to earning an AA in art. Jordan's creative goal is to provide companionship for the viewer and to prompt the viewer to think introspectively.

Slave is a resident of Citrus Heights, California. He has had three art pieces shown at American River College. He would like to show his pieces in galleries, but is otherwise uncertain as to where he wants to go with his art.

Simon Tafoya is a first-time featured artist to the *American River Review* with his piece *Nymph*.

Edris Tauber lives in Citrus Heights, California. Edris's work has appeared in the 2012 and 2013 editions of the *American River Review* and has also appeared in several local gallery shows.

Jessica Tietjen is from Sacramento, California and holds a BFA in studio art from Humboldt State University. She is the owner of Urban Canopy Eco-Art Studio and works to connect her audience with her love of the natural world through her art.

Ulysses Unzueta is a Sacramento, California resident working toward building his own artistic style. He aims to absorb as much as possible from school, fellow artists, and different art mediums.

Zach Winn is currently studying to transfer. He has experience in the film and gaming industries, and his work has been featured at downtown Sacramento galleries. His artistic focus concentrates on a person's inner life, whether quiet or dramatic, to reveal humanity through art.

Yuk Mui Michelle Wong is from Sacramento, California. Her artwork has appeared in the 2013 and 2014 editions of the *American River Review*. Inspired by a love of organic forms, she creates with the hope that her art puts the viewer in a joyful mood.

Elizabeth Xedes lives in Roseville, California. She recently received the Harris Award from the DSPS Art Show, and her goal as an artist is to continue to be inspired and create art that will inspire others.

Nancy Z'berg-Jennings is a resident of Orangevale, California. Winner of the 2013 Kingsley Award, she explores dream imagery, spiritual symbolism, and myth through her figurative sculptures. One of her pieces was shown at the Blue Moon Gallery.

Sarah Martinez is a resident of Sacramento, California, who has been making ceramic art for seventeen years. She has participated in shows at Sacramento City College, E Street Gallery, and Sol Ceramica Clay Studio, and is currently taking classes at both Sacramento City College and American River College.

Armin Masoumi is from Carmichael, California. Armin has a 3D animation certificate and has hopes of one day owning a studio called Sofal for animation, game publishing, and visual effects editing.

Maren McCallister is a Midwest transplant currently residing near the American River in Rancho Cordova, California. Maren holds a MFA and has worked twenty-five years as a designer, including five years designing exhibits and museums in Australia as an interpretive ranger. Maren is now studying fine arts from a new perspective and is rekindling her professional interests in photography and mixed media.

Thomas McFall resides in North Highlands, California. In 2013, he received his AA in art new media and was the Art Director for the 2014 edition of the *American River Review*. He plans to finish his BS in graphic design at CSU, Sacramento, after which he hopes to share his designs with those in the Sacramento area.

Philip Morgan is a high school graduate who lives in North Highlands, California. His goal as an artist is to create and animate those characters and stories that have thus far existed only in his head and on paper.

David Navarro resides in Fair Oaks, California and has his masters of performing arts. He is currently working toward a certificate from American River College. He works to perfect his craft in portal photography, time art photography, and landscape photography with 3D application.

Eva Mae Natividad lives in Sacramento, California. She has her BS in neurobiology, physiology, and behavior from UC Davis. She won honorable mention at the fall group show *Sharada* at E Street Gallery. An aspiring medical illustrator, Eva Mae is drawn to create realistic, observational pieces. She feels that science and art both demand refined observational skills, and that her personal style captures light and color.

Susan Poirier juried the KME Art Auction from 2010-2013, and in 2011 won the Juror's Award for Contemporary Classics in the KVIE Art Auction. Her art was also featured in the 2010 and the 2012 editions of the *American River Review*. Susan would like to inspire people's curiosity and reflective moments while they view her work.

Kaia Sanfilippo lives in Shingle Springs, California. She graduated from American River College in Spring 2014 with an AA in art new media. She aspires to become a concept artist in the video game and animation industry, and will perhaps run a web comic on the side.

Cecelia Sayer is from Carmichael, California. She was featured in the 2005 *American River Review* and won 3rd place in ceramic sculpture in the 2004 Student Art Commotion.

Melanie Scott is a resident of Sacramento, California. She has been commissioned as an artist since high school and helped paint a mural in the Natomas School District office. Inspired by her love for cartoons, she plans to major in animation and hopes to work

Kyle Doka is a resident of Carmichael, California. He earned a BFA in drawing from Arizona State University. He hopes to earn his MFA and become a professional photographer.

Graham Fredenburg is from Carmichael, California. He has taken several art courses which allowed him to incorporate natural elements into his work. He is constantly trying to push the limits of his skill by exploring new possibilities with various mediums.

Michael Fullilove is a resident of Citrus Heights, California. Since a young age, he has been inspired by visual storytelling. In his time at American River College, he discovered his passion for character design and animation. In the future he hopes to create and develop memorable characters for films or video games.

Antony Galvan lives in Sacramento, California. Over the years he has accomplished much: designing for a San Francisco business in the 1980s and '90s, holding a solo show at the Muddy Waters Café, being published in the *American River Review* and the American River College 2014 Calendar, and graduating from ITT Technical Institute. He is currently enrolled at ARC in the hopes of obtaining an AA.

Genesys lives in Antelope, California. Her goal as an artist is threefold: to raise consciousness about current world issues, inspire viewers to imagine different worlds, and provoke a vivid emotional reaction.

Jeannie Sou Hall is a first-time featured artist to the *American River Review* with three untitled pieces.

Penny Hanscom is from Carmichael, California. She has her AA in studio art from American River College. She has participated in many local, national, and international shows and won many awards. Her goal is to share artistic creations that others will enjoy.

Jonathan Horcasitas is a resident of Sacramento, California. He was published in the 2014 *American River Review*, as well as in UCLA's magazine, *La Gente*. His goal is to make cartoons.

Sue Kelly is a native of Fresno who now resides in Folsom, California, where she has her own studio. She has earned an AA and her art has been shown with the Folsom Arts Association and in the James Kaneko Gallery. Her goal as an artist is to capture in clay the inner beauty of animals.

Denise Kibbe-Phillips is a resident of Citrus Heights, California. She hopes to work in all different mediums and extend her skill set into the 3D fields of sculpture, metal, ceramic, glass, and woodblock. She also wishes to open a studio where she can show and sell her work.

Victoria Kozycz has shown her work in various galleries and has been published in *Photographer's Forum* magazine's "Best of College Photography," earning honorable mention in 2009 and finalist in 2011. She takes her main inspiration from nature, whether from its shadows and contours, the smallest of creatures, or the blunt realities of the natural world.

Amy K. Larson lives in Orangevale, California. In 2013, she had her work shown at the American River College Student Art Show in the James Kaneko Gallery. She hopes to one day own a studio and gallery and have a small photography and design business.

Kyla Lewis is a resident of Sacramento, California. She hopes to pursue a career in commercial illustration or teaching.

Paja Lynhiavue is from Sacramento, California and has shown her work at American River College's James Kaneko Gallery. Paja believes that art can be made from anything and hopes to travel overseas and teach art to those who do not have the luxury of being in the presence of it.

Art Contributors

Louis Archuleta is an artist from Sacramento, California. He is currently attending American River College to obtain his photography certificate. His main objective in his work is to capture the viewer's imagination and the rare and unique moments in everyday life.

Dakota Arguello is a Fair Oaks, California native and returning featured artist from the 2014 *American River Review*. In 2013, he also had his work featured in *Sharada*, a student art show at the E Street Gallery, and has been a Chalk-It-Up participant since 2003. Dakota's goal as an artist is to explore the relationship between an object or person and the space in which they dwell.

Cathie Bechtell is from Cameron Park, California. She earned a degree in art new media at American River College with a 4.0 GPA. She was recently awarded Best 2D in Show at the Fine Arts Student Show. Her pieces have appeared in juried and non-juried exhibitions. Cathie decided to further her art education later in life after a career in technical drawing and drafting. She was previously published in the 2013 *American River Review*.

Matthew Beltran is from Rio Linda, California. He is an art new media major who is persistent in his pursuit to both broaden his horizon as an artist and to exceed perceived limitations. He lives by the motto, "Learn what there is to be learned!"

Hanna Benedychuk is a resident of North Highlands, California. She has particapated in several individual and group art exhibitions featured in venues such as the Crocker Art Museum and the James Kaneko Gallery. She strives to make her work come alive and thrives on trying to be the kind of artist that can change somebody's life through her work.

Liam Byrd-Smith is from Carmichael, California and was published in the 2014 *American River Review*. His goals are to make beautiful art and to one day be a professional artist.

Erica Campbell is a Citrus Heights, California native who was featured in the 2014 *American River Review*. She was also featured in the James Kaneko Gallery's Community Shows from 2011 to 2013. Her ultimate goals are to develop enough skill in various mediums to free her imagination and to help others feel comfortable expressing themselves through art.

Cheri is a resident of Sacramento, California. She is currently in her first semester at American River College. Her dream is to create art that makes the world a better place.

Christl Clinton is from Citrus Heights, California. In 2013, she had several pieces of her work featured in various galleries. She puts a heavy emphasis on using an alternative process to show the true beauty of the world through a camera lens.

Contra lives in Sacramento, California. His goal as an artist is to create an original style with original concepts that will inspire others.

J. Costa lives in Sacramento, California and is an art major at American River College hoping to transfer to a university and study abroad in Italy. Jackie sold three pieces of her artwork last fall.

Jude Croxford is from Sacramento, California. In 2013, her painting *Panic* won best 2D work of art in a student show. She plans on earning her certificate in illustration this year from American River College. Jude will continue to paint in oils and use digital media to expand her body of work.

Gallery Staff

Art Selection
Liam Byrd-Smith (S14)
Jacqueline Costa (S14)
Brian Ford (S14)
Miguel Gonzalez (S14)
Donald Gough (S14)
Stephan Henderson (S14)
Danielle Keith (S14)
Larissa Kimmey (S14)
Oleg Klyushnik (S14)
Maren McCallister (S14)
Katherine McCoy (S14)
Tashelle Miller (S14)
Cynthia Monk (S14)
Philip Morgan (S14)
Nathan Reynolds (S14)
Zachary Winn (S14)

Gallery Layout
Tiffani Evans (F14)
Larissa Kimmey (F14)

Art New Media Staff

Faculty Advisers
Craig Martinez (F14)
Betty Nelsen (S14)
Jeff Rochford (F14)

Art Director
Amanda Layng-Martinez (F14)

Cover Artists
Susan Negrete (F14)
Rachel Story (F14)

Designers
Sondra Ames-Hauger (F14)
Brian Ford (F14)
Amy K. Larson (F14)
Kaylee Mulholland (F14)
Susan Negrete (F14)
Amber Padilla (F14)
Rachel Story (F14)

Fashion Layout
Sam Collier (F14)
Saul Ramirez Latvanen (F14)

Photographer
Macie Vang (F14)

Production Manager
Tashelle Miller (F14)

Production Team
Tysen Cannady (F14)
Jalen Conner (F14)
Bryant Eckart (F14)
Miguel Gonzalez (F14)
Jaimi Gotro (F14)
Philip Morgan (F14)
Charlie Norwood (F14)
Jorge Riley (F14)
Angela Velasquez (F14)
Porter Womble (F14)

Fashion In Motion

Studio 105

ARC Fashion Team

Stylist: **Saul Latvanen**
Assistant Stylist: **Sam Collier**
Photographer: **Macie Vang**

Hair Stylist: **Henadzi Harbaruk** of Golden Hands
Make up Artist: **Karina Martin**

Models: **Cheyenne Jorgenson, Amanda Visger, Brianna Staffler, Angy Suastegui, Bailey McWhorther, Fatima Ramirez, Ricardo Pina, Marquis Youngblood, Robert Tangipa**

Best of Show: **Rebeka Garn**
Best Construction: **Helen Romero**
Most Marketable: **Hagen Valencia**
Most Creative: **Joshua Earle**

Hagen Valencia believes fashion should be practical and adapt well to daily life. His collection **"Into the Abyss"** embodies the dark elements and rebellious spirit of street soul, though Hagen also conveys a feeling of hope with contrasting flashes of light. Hagen is inspired by his extensive work within the retail industry, and he aspires to run his own boutique.

Helen Romero introduces **"Lilly Belle,"** a ready-to-wear summer collection for girls, ages 5 to 7. Imagined as the wardrobe of a princess, the pastel-hued dresses showcase the designer's talent for intricately detailed handwork. Helen's greatest inspiration is her mother, who was also a gifted seamstress. Helen surely has a bright future in design.

Shape, tailoring, color, and contrast are integral elements in the designs of **Joshua Earle**. His collection **"British Invasion"** is an edgy blend of couture meets punk. Joshua is inspired by historical silhouettes, and updates these in bold, modern, detailed designs that always bring a splash of excitement to the runway. Joshua hopes to intern in Europe and to eventually work for a design house.

Rebeka Garn draws her inspiration from many sources, and adds her personal interpretation through her skilled use of color and texture. Her collection **"Fawned of You"** was inspired by deer frolicking in nature. Her use of neutral colors with pastel details are feminine and delicate, while at the same time, confident and assured. The classic combination of fitted bodices with flowing skirts is updated with sheer, natural fabrics. This is just the beginning for Rebeka.